Fortress • 17

D1706315

OSPREY
PUBLISHING

Troy *c.* 1700–1250 BC

D1706316

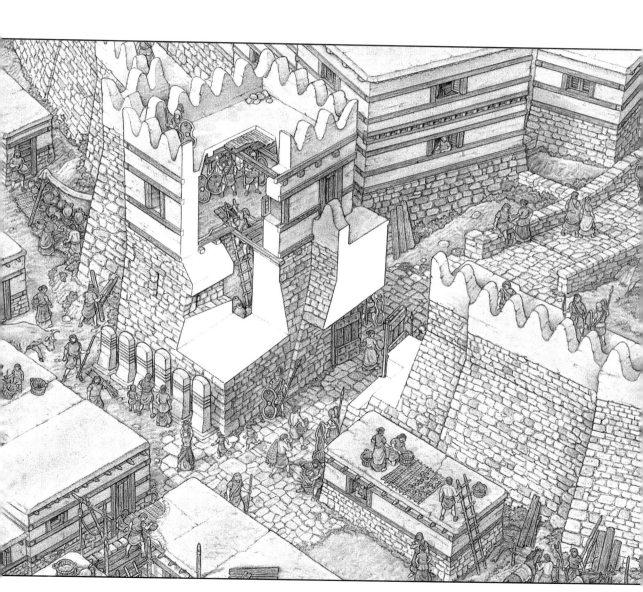

Nic Fields • Illustrated by D Spedaliere & S Sulemsohn Spedaliere

Series editors Marcus Cowper and Nikolai Bogdanovic

First published in Great Britain in 2004 by Osprey Publishing, Elms Court, Chapel Way, Botley, Oxford OX2 9LP, United Kingdom.
Email: info@ospreypublishing.com

ISBN 1 84176 703 4

Editorial by Ilios Publishing, Oxford, UK (www.iliospublishing.com)
Maps by The Map Studio, Romsey, UK
Index by David Worthington
Design: Ken Vail Graphic Design, Cambridge, UK
Originated by The Electronic Page Company, Cwmbran, UK
Printed and bound by L-Rex Printing Company Ltd.

04 05 06 07 08   10 9 8 7 6 5 4 3 2

A CIP catalogue record for this book is available from the British Library.

FOR A CATALOGUE OF ALL BOOKS PUBLISHED BY OSPREY MILITARY AND AVIATION PLEASE CONTACT:

Osprey Direct USA, c/o MBI Publishing, PO Box 1, 729 Prospect Ave, Osceola, WI 54020, USA.
Email: info@ospreydirectusa.com

Osprey Direct UK, PO Box 140, Wellingborough, Northants, NN8 2FA, United Kingdom.
Email: info@ospreydirect.co.uk

www.ospreypublishing.com

Artist's note

Our sincere thanks to all who have helped in the preparation of this book. We would like to dedicate this book to our dearest daughter Alina.

Readers may care to note that the original paintings from which the colour plates in this book were prepared are available for private sale. All reproduction copyright whatsoever is retained by the Publishers. All enquiries should be addressed to:

Sarah Sulemsohn
Tel-Fax: 00 39 0575 692210
info@alinaillustrazioni.com
alina@alinaillustrazioni.com
www.alinaillustrazioni.com

The Publishers regret that they can enter into no correspondence upon this matter.

Editor's note

When classical authors are referred to throughout the text the standard form of reference has been adopted. The formula used is 'author', 'title' (if the author wrote more than one work) followed by a one-, two- or three-figure reference. If the work is a play or poem, the figure reference indicates either 'line' or 'book' and 'line'. Thus 'Homer (*Odyssey* 8.512)' refers to line 512 of the eighth book of the *Odyssey*. Alternatively, if the work is a treatise, the figure reference indicates 'book' and 'chapter' or 'book', 'chapter' and 'paragraph'. Thus 'Strabo (13.1.32)' refers to paragraph 32 of chapter 1 of the 13th book of the only surviving work by Strabo. When modern authors are referred to throughout the text the Harvard system of referencing has been adopted. The formula used is 'author', 'publication date' followed by page number(s). Thus 'Drews (1993: 106)' refers to page 106 of his 1993 publication, that is, *The End of the Bronze Age: Changes in Warfare and the Catastrophe c. 1200 BC*.

Contents

Introduction

Hisarlik, the 'place of the fort', is a small site, a sandy stone-strewn mound cut up into gullies and hummocks. Troy, however, is immense. Its story sprawls across cultures, time and geography. In 1820, in an essay for the *Edinburgh Review*, Charles Maclaren (1782–1866), the Scottish traveller and founder-editor of *The Scotsman*, wrote:

> Ilium was for a considerable period to the Heathen World, what Jerusalem is now to the Christian, a 'sacred' city which attracted pilgrims by the fame of its wars and woes, and by the shadow of ancient sanctity reposing upon it. (*Edinburgh Review*, 1863: 222)

Out of all the stories told by humankind and recorded through its turbulent history, the tale of the sack of Troy is perhaps the greatest secular story ever told. It has certainly captured the western imagination for some 3,000 years.

Despite the problems inherent in any attempt to employ Greek myths, oral traditions and, above all, the Homeric epics in a historical reconstruction of the Trojan War, recent evidence from in and around the site of Troy has prompted many scholars to take a fresh look at the 'Homeric Question'. Although the literary and historical record, which make up the background to the tale of Troy, will be touched upon, the focus of this brief work is not centred on Homer and history. On the contrary, its aim is to outline the history of the fortifications of Troy, covering in some detail the walls of Troy VI, and their correlation to the destruction of the site by the Mycenaean Greeks.

Marble bust of Homer, a Roman copy of a lost Greek sculpture of the 2nd century BC, found in the Theatre of Dionysios, Athens. Although the ancient Greeks believed that the great epics, the *Iliad* and the *Odyssey*, were the work of the poet Homer, reliable information about the poet's life was as elusive then as it is today. This sculpture, therefore, is not a real portrait but a conceptual image of creative genius. The unruly hair and knitted brow suggest intensity and passion. The worn, furrowed face reflects experience. The eyes, sightless in accordance with ancient tradition, reflect the belief that Homer and other great bards saw into the future and beyond this world. (Author's Collection)

Chronology of major Bronze Age events

Please note that all chronological dates must be taken as circa not absolute.

3100	Start of Bronze Age culture on mainland Greece, Cyclades and Crete
3100–1900	Minoan Pre-Palatial period on Crete (EM I–III & MM IA)
2900	Hisarlik is settled and soon fortified (Troy I)
2600	Start of Cycladic culture in the Cyclades
2450	Troy Ik destroyed but soon rebuilt (Troy IIa)
1900–1700	Minoan Proto-Palatial period on Crete (MM IB–IIB)
1700–1450	Minoan Neo-Palatial period on Crete (MM III–LM IB)
1700–1250	Troy VI, established by Neo-Trojans, major trade centre and maritime power
1650–1550	Grave Circle B at Mycenae (LH I)
1650	Foundation of Hattušas-Boğazköy by Hattušili I
1628	Cataclysmic eruption of Thera (Santorini) according to scientists
1600	Cyclades under Minoan influence
1550–1425	Grave Circle A at Mycenae (LH I– IIB)
1500	Cataclysmic eruption of Thera according to archaeologists
1457	Battle of Meggido
1450	Mycenaeans at Knossos, Crete (Linear B) and in Cyclades
1380	Destruction of Knossos
1300	Treasury of Atreus at Mycenae (LH IIIB)
1275	Battle of Kadesh
1260/50	Destruction of Troy VIh (Homer's Troy?)
1250	Lion Gate at Mycenae (LH IIIB); Tawagalawas Letter written by Hattušili III
1200	Warrior Vase from Mycenae (LH IIIB/C)
1200/1180	Widespread destruction of Mycenaean palaces (LH IIIB/C)
1190/80	Destruction of Hattušas-Boğazköy
1185	Destruction of Ugarit
1184	Traditional date for destruction of Homer's Troy according to Herodotos
1180	Destruction of Troy VIIa
1179	Ramesses III defeats the 'Peoples of the Sea' in the Nile Delta
1100	So-called invasion of Dorian Greeks from north-west Greece
1050	Migration of mainland Greeks to Aegean islands and Anatolia

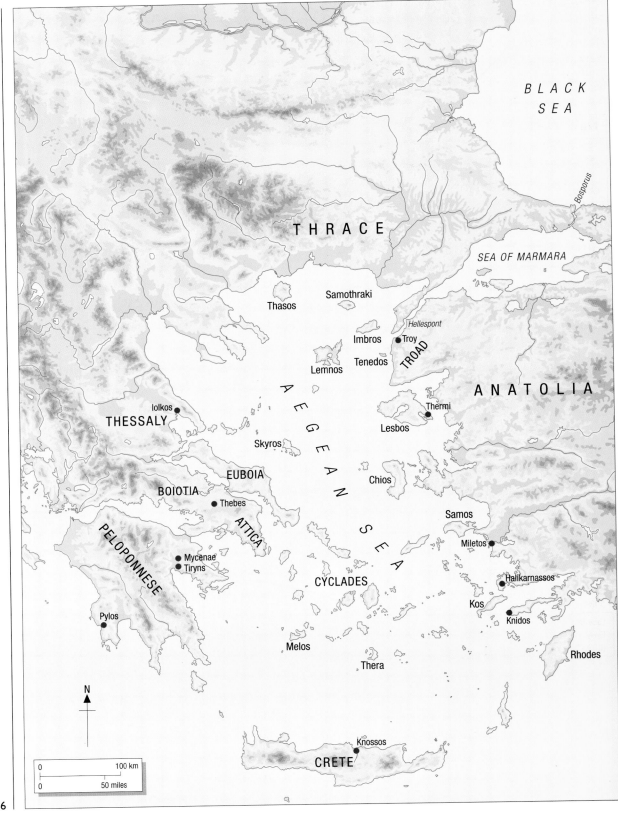

BLACK SEA

THRACE

SEA OF MARMARA

Bosporus

Samothraki

Thasos

Hellespont

Imbros

Troy

TROAD

Tenedos

ANATOLIA

Lemnos

A E G E A N

Thermi

Iolkos

Lesbos

THESSALY

Skyros

EUBOIA

Chios

BOIOTIA

Thebes

S E A

Samos

ATTICA

Miletos

PELOPONNESE

Mycenae

Tiryns

CYCLADES

Halikarnassos

Kos

Knidos

Pylos

Melos

Rhodes

Thera

N

0   100 km

0   50 miles

Knossos

CRETE

6

Aegean Bronze Age chronology

All dates are approximate, not absolute, and come almost entirely from two sources, namely radiocarbon dates and artefacts. The artefacts are those foreign objects of reasonably secure date found in archaeologically sound Aegean contexts, and Aegean objects (whose relative date in Aegean contexts is secure) found as imports in foreign (mainly Egyptian) contexts whose date does not depend entirely on a relative cultural sequence.

OPPOSITE The Aegean in the Late Bronze Age, the world of the Mycenaeans, the Trojans and the Hittites, three peoples at the apogee of their respective powers.

Near East	Mainland Greece	Dates
Early Bronze Age (EBA)	Early Helladic (EH)	c. 2900–2000 BC
Middle Bronze Age (MBA)	Middle Helladic (MH)	c. 2000–1650 BC
Late Bronze Age (LBA)	Late Helladic (LH)	c. 1650–1050 BC
PROTO-PALATIAL PERIOD LH I, IIA & IIB	Grave Circles A & B, Mycenae	c. 1650–1425 BC
PALATIAL PERIOD LH IIIA & IIIB LH IIIB/C	Mycenaean palace complexes Palace destruction levels	c. 1425–1200 BC c. 1200 BC
POST-PALATIAL PERIOD LH IIIC Sub-Mycenaean	Transition to Iron Age	c. 1190–1050 BC c. 1050–1000 BC

Trojan Bronze Age chronology

The Trojan sequence has long been known, first exposed by Schliemann, then revised and refined in later excavations conducted by the University of Cincinnati under Blegen. Recently new C-14 samples have been taken from the site of Troy itself, which may result in changes to the dates of Troy I–V, but nothing of a substantial nature. The new excavation by Korfmann may yield further revisions.

ANATOLIA	TROY	STRATA	DATES
Early Bronze Age II (EBI/EB II)	Maritime Troia Culture I	Troy Ia–Ik	c. 2900–2450 BC
Early Bronze Age II (EB II)	Maritime Troia Culture II	Troy IIa–IIh	c. 2450–2200 BC
Early Bronze Age III to Middle Bronze Age (EB III–MBA)	Maritime Troia Culture III Anatolian Troia Culture I Anatolian Troia Culture II	Troy IIIa–IIId Troy IVa–IVe Troy Va–Vd	c. 2200–1700 BC
Middle Bronze Age to Late Bronze Age (MBA–LBA)	High Troia Culture I	Troy VIa–VIh	c. 1700–1250 BC
Late Bronze Age to Early Iron Age (LBA–EIA)	High Troia Culture II	Troy VIIa–VIIb2	c. 1250–1050 BC

The story so far

The story of the archaeological quest for the historical reality behind Homer's *Iliad* and *Odyssey* is almost as epic as the tales themselves, and any account of archaeological Troy, the Troy that was built by men, of stone, mud and timber, must surely open with Heinrich Schliemann (1822–90). In every sense, Schliemann was a man of colossal energy. He was a consummate businessman, who had made several fortunes for himself. He brought gold dust from the miners in Sacramento, sold potassium nitrate to the Russian Army during the Crimean War, dealt in commodities in St Petersburg, acquired and rented prime property in Paris, invested in American and Cuban railways and Brazilian bonds, to name but a few of his commercial activities. He could speak and write fluently in more than a dozen languages, including Greek and Russian. He knew large sections of the Koran (in Arabic) by heart. But it is not for these achievements that he is world famous.

A burning ambition

In 1829, when he was eight years old, Schliemann was captivated by the stories of the Trojan War and resolved that one day he would excavate Troy. He devoted the early part of his life to commerce in order to earn enough money to be able to realise his childhood dream. At last, in his mid-40s, he went to the Sorbonne in Paris to study archaeology. On a trip to the plain of Troy in 1868 he reached, on the mound of Hisarlik, the momentous decision that here, not at Pinarbaşi, as most scholars then believed, was the site of Homer's Troy. Soon after this he set about proving his theory by the evidence of his spade – the first seeker of Troy to take this practical step. His theory received dramatic confirmation at the end of May 1873, when, with the help of his wife Sophia, he discovered a large treasure next to the city wall, which he called 'Priam's Treasure'. In August 1876 at Mycenae, again with the help of his wife, Schliemann excavated golden death masks and masses of other treasure from the Shaft Graves. In one of the graves

Schliemann's final resting-place, located in the First Cemetery, Athens, is a fitting expression of the man's character and his life's work. Schliemann's mausoleum, which he designed himself, is a miniature Doric temple whose decorative friezes show him and his wife, Sophia, excavating at Troy and Mycenae. The inscription above the entrance, which is a powerful declaration of how he wanted to be remembered, simply says HEROI SCHLIMANNOI ('For the hero Schliemann'). At the front of the mausoleum, Schliemann's bust sits directly above an image of King Proitos directing the Cyclopes to build the towering walls of Tiryns. The intention is quite clear. The viewer is to draw a parallel between the founder of Tiryns, the future birthplace of Herakles, and Schliemann, who directed the excavations of Troy and Mycenae. (Author's collection)

he found a mummy wearing a gold mask, which he removed and, finding the remains of a human face underneath, promptly declared in a telegram to the Hellenic minister of education, 'I have gazed upon the face of Agamemnon.' The gold death mask he called the 'Mask of Agamemnon', and it is still known by that name.

These highlights form part of the essential picture of Schliemann, as scholars and the general public alike know him. Recent research, however, has shown that every statement in the preceding paragraph is false.

It is often said that we know so much about Troy today because of one man's obsession, indeed of his childhood dreams, which he made come true. However, this is only so if we can believe Schliemann's personal account of his early life. Schliemann's is the most romantic story in archaeology and should be read with a very large pinch of salt for with Schliemann, as with the story of Troy, it is not always possible to distinguish myth from reality. Addicted to hyperbole, braggadocio and often downright lies, Schliemann, the German merchant prince-turned-keen-archaeologist, presents us with the curious paradox of being at once the 'father of archaeology' and a teller of tall stories. For deep down Schliemann desperately craved the respect and admiration of the academic world as a serious scholar and archaeologist and, on top of this, he was a romantic philhellene. Schliemann's psyche was a bundle of contradictions.

Golden Troy

In truth it was his chance meeting with Frank Calvert that gave Schliemann the inspiration to turn to archaeology and the idea of discovering Homer's Troy by excavation. Although Charles Maclaren deserves the first credit for identifying Hisarlik as Troy, it was the Englishman Calvert who was the first on the settlement-mound in 1865. Although he served as the US vice-consul in Çanakkale, Calvert was also a keen antiquarian who had purchased the eastern half of Hisarlik. It was here that he immediately uncovered the remains of the temple of Athena and the walls of Lysimachos (r. 301–280 BC), the splendid Hellenistic defences the remains of which were to be swept away by Schliemann. Calvert also struck Bronze Age levels and realised Hisarlik was deeply stratified. Schliemann, on the other hand, first visited the Troad (Greek *Troias*, the 'land of Troy') in August 1868 and Hisarlik made no impression on him. It was only when he met Calvert at Çanakkale on his way back to Istanbul that he heard details of Calvert's excavation and his theory that Hisarlik was an artificial mound where 'the rubbish and debris of habitations had been thrown down … for centuries' (Schliemann 1880: 40). Calvert immediately convinced Schliemann that this was the site of Homer's Troy.

Schliemann's excavation of Troy was, by modern standards, impatient and brutal. With his new Greek bride, the 17-year-old Sophia Engasteromenos, he conducted a preliminary excavation in April 1870, and from 1871 to 1873 he made three major campaigns totalling over nine months' work with anything from 80 to 160 workmen, equipped only with spades, on the site each day. Schliemann's aim was to drive a vast trench through the mound from the north, removing hundreds of tons of earth and rubble and demolishing later structures that stood in his way. He had come to

Schliemann's 'Great Trench', which was driven from north to south through the settlement-mound of Hisarlik, is the result of his initial excavations. This view is looking north, and exposed in the bottom are the stone foundations, built in 'herringbone' technique, of some of the close-set long houses of Troy I. While his early methods were crude and destroyed a lot of valuable data, Schliemann did learn as he went, and later excavators were able to piece together the complex history of Troy, which contains many strata and sub-strata. (Author's collection)

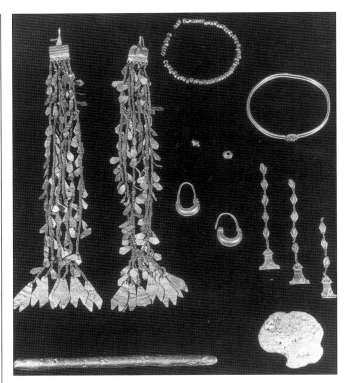

the conclusion that Homer's Troy was the second city from the bottom (Troy II), which had been destroyed in a great conflagration and was thus labelled as the 'Burnt City'. On 31 May 1873, Schliemann found 'Priam's Treasure'. Sophia was not present, as her husband later alleged; she was not even in Turkey. Smuggled out of Turkey, this golden horde was later housed in the Ethnographic Museum in Berlin, from where it mysteriously disappeared during the dying days of the Third Reich. Recently, however, 'Priam's Treasure' has come to light. Ever since April 1945, when it was taken by a Red Army 'Trophy Brigade', it has been tucked away in the Pushkin State Museum of Fine Arts in Moscow.

Schliemann was to return to Hisarlik for two further major campaigns during 1878–79, and for another season in 1882 with Wilhelm Dörpfeld (1853–1940), an architectural historian who soon clarified the mess Schliemann had left from the earlier campaigns. The period 1889 to 1890 was his last season and it was then that he discovered the ruins of a 'megaron-style' building belonging to Troy VI outside the great ramp of Troy II, which he believed the Trojans had used to bring in the Wooden Horse inside their walls. To Schliemann's dismay Troy II had flourished over 1,000 years earlier than the alleged time of the Trojan War, c. 2450–2200 BC. It was Dörpfeld who, between 1893 and 1894, unearthed Troy VI and its impressive cut-stone fortification-walls, some 4.5m thick with their distinctive batter and lofty towers, including the massive north-east bastion. German and Turkish archaeologists believe that this wealthy and well-fortified settlement was the Troy of Priam.

Schliemann's and Dörpfeld's work was later carried on by C. W. Blegen (1887–1971) – who believed Troy VIIa was Homer's city and not Troy VIh – and archaeologists from the University of Cincinnati. Blegen's dig at Troy lasted seven seasons between 1932 and 1938 and it was a model excavation for its day. Schliemann's, Dörpfeld's and Blegen's combined efforts have revealed 46 levels of occupation and nine 'cities', dating from c. 2900–2450 BC to c. AD 550, one of which may have been the 'well-walled city' of the *Iliad*.

Old tales, new thoughts

Increasingly, modern scholars are prepared to believe that something like the Trojan War really took place – possibly around 1250 BC – and was one of a number of forays by Mycenaean Greeks against the shores of western Anatolia. During the last 20 years a number of important discoveries have cast fresh light on the old tales, thereby opening the way for a substantial reappraisal of the archaeology of Homeric Troy.

In 1982, on the coast 8km south-west of Troy, German archaeologists under Manfred Korfmann of Universität Tübingen began to excavate an extensive Late Bronze Age burial site near the conical mound of Beşik Tepe and within a few metres of what was then a sheltered sandy beach. The cemetery, which the ancients regarded as the Tomb of Achilles, alluded to by Homer (*Iliad* 23.126), evidently known to Strabo (13.1.32) and the scene of visits by Alexander the Great (Arrian *Anabasis* 1.12.1), Mehmet the Conqueror (Kritoboulos 4.11.5) and Lord Byron (Letter to Henry Drury, 3 May 1810), was composed of some 200 burials surrounded by a perimeter wall. It does not appear to relate to any permanent settlement in the immediate area.

Many of the burials were in large *pithoi* laid on their sides, with their mouths covered by stone slabs. Remains of men, women and children were identified. Some had been cremated, while others had been inhumed. Over 50 of the burials contained imported Mycenaean goods together with material indigenous to the Troad, with pottery indicating a date on the borderline between Troy VIh and

Arrowheads and spearheads, along with sling bullets, found in the destruction level of Troy VIh. Korfmann's excavation, as did Dörpfeld's, revealed signs of war, namely a charcoal layer dated roughly to 1250 BC, and bronze spearheads and arrowheads scattered in the debris and lodged in the fortification-walls. (Turkish Ministry of Education, photograph M. Gülbiz)

Troy VIIa, the likely period of the Trojan War. At the centre of this burial complex stood a substantial grave-house (Tomb 15) measuring some 4 by 3m, with a *pithos* in its inner chamber containing the remains of three separate cremations. Fragments of bronze objects that could have been swords or daggers were also recovered. The grave goods here included a fine Mycenaean *krater*, a terracotta vessel used for mixing wine and water, together with fragments of gold jewellery, remnants of the rich contents, which had been looted by robbers after the cemetery was abandoned. A large storage vessel, or *pithos*, in the porch of the grave-house yielded the first Mycenaean seal-stone to be found *in situ* in Anatolia, a lentoid seal of black stone with the representation of a 'human' face. It seems reasonable to infer that Korfmann's cemetery provides evidence of mercantile, and possibly also military, activity by Mycenaeans in close proximity to Troy at or about the time of Troy VIh. In other words, his finds have an important bearing on the Trojan War of Greek tradition.

Korfmann transferred his attentions to Troy itself in 1988 and a larger international team made up of German, American and Turkish specialists has been operating there since that date. Project Troia, as it is officially known, is an enormous enterprise with over 100 archaeologists who, along with more traditional procedures, make extensive use of modern scientific and technological methods. One of the most notable findings of the project is that the plateau lying just south of the mound and citadel of Hisarlik was a densely inhabited area, not only in the time of Graeco-Roman Troy (*Novum Ilium*), but also in the Late Bronze Age. This area, then, was the lower town of Laomedon's and Priam's Troy and was protected by its own circuit-wall. The magnetometer has revealed the line of this extended fortification curving round to join the monumental walls of Troy VI.

Homer's Troy has now been revealed as one of the largest fortified sites of the entire Bronze Age, on a par with Hattušas-Boğazköy or Mycenae. In one stroke, the area of the fortified *enceinte* has been increased from some 20,000 to around 270,000 m^2 (*c.* 27ha). What Schliemann discovered was just the upper citadel of a much larger settlement. Schliemann was always troubled by the comparative smallness of the Troy he knew, especially as Homer had painted it as a grand metropolis with towering ramparts.

Mycenaean lentoid seal of black stone with the representation of a 'human' face from Tomb 15, Beşik Tepe cemetery. This is the first Mycenaean seal-stone to be found *in situ* in Anatolia. (Reproduced from Korfmann, M., et al., *Traum und Wirklichkeit: Troia*, Theiss, Stuttgart, 2001)

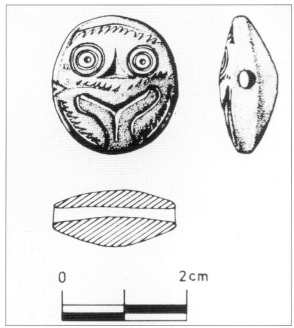

0   2 cm

The nine 'cities' of Troy

What is now an inconspicuous bluff scarred by heaps of spoil and debris, the settlement-mound of Hisarlik came into being through a happy combination of circumstances. First, its favourable location on a limestone spur projecting into a shallow marine embayment, long since silted up, caused it to be reoccupied time and again for some 3,500 years. Second, mud-brick was largely used for building the walls of the houses. The most convenient and serviceable of all substances for low-cost construction clay, in the form of sun-dried bricks scarcely known in Europe, was and still is the traditional building material in the Near East. When building took place, the mud-bricks from previous structures were of no value and buildings of the preceding phase were always levelled. Thus a raised site, or tell, gradually grew up. The bottom seven layers of the settlement-mound, Troy I–VII, contain the remains of 42 building phases belonging to the Bronze Age. On top of these come the remains of Greek (Troy VIII) and Roman (Troy IX) constructions. Altogether the process produced an artificial accumulation of earth that is some 20m high.

Location and landscape

The settlement-mound of Hisarlik occupies the western tip of a low limestone ridge running eastward from Mount Ida (Kaz Dağ), between the alluvial plain of the Skamander (Karamenderes) to the south and the marshy valley of the Simois (Dümrek-Su) to the north. This ridge, which in the Bronze Age was a sea-girt headland, ends somewhat abruptly in steep slopes on the north and west and a more gradual descent toward the south. Some four miles distant westward beyond a low range of hills, and across what was once the bay in front of Troy, is the Aegean Sea. To the north and less than an hour's walk away is the Hellespont, the narrow straits now called the Dardanelles, with the steep cliffs along the Gallipoli peninsula rising in the background, a region rich in historical associations from ancient to modern times. Controlling navigation between the Black Sea and the Mediterranean, the Dardanelles have long been of immense strategic and commercial importance.

Troy lies at the point where East and West, the Black Sea and the Mediterranean all meet – a location very favourable to trade and ideal as a centre of power. Maintaining a strategic maritime advantage due to its position at the opening of the Dardanelles, it also controlled a land route that came up along the western coastal region of Anatolia to the shortest crossing of the

An aerial view, looking north-west, shows the ruins of the citadel of Troy on Hisarlik. Originally an oval-shaped mound, it now bears the deep scares and dumps of more than 30 seasons of archaeological investigation. In the second millennium BC the fertile litoral plain at the top of the photograph was shallow sea, which formed a marine embayment just south of the entrance to the Dardanelles. (H. Oge, *Atlas*, Heft 78, September 1999)

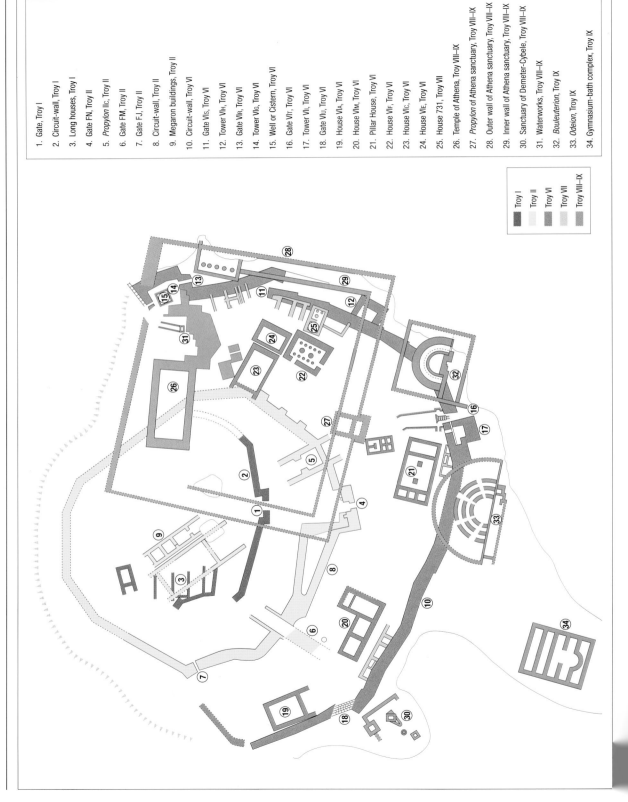

1. Gate, Troy I
2. Circuit-wall, Troy I
3. Long houses, Troy I
4. Gate FN, Troy II
5. *Propylon* IIc, Troy II
6. Gate FM, Troy II
7. Gate FJ, Troy II
8. Circuit-wall, Troy II
9. Megaron buildings, Troy II
10. Circuit-wall, Troy VI
11. Gate VIs, Troy VI
12. Tower VIh, Troy VI
13. Gate VIr, Troy VI
14. Tower VIg, Troy VI
15. Well or Cistern, Troy VI
16. Gate VIt, Troy VI
17. Tower VII, Troy VI
18. Gate VIu, Troy VI
19. House VIa, Troy VI
20. House VIm, Troy VI
21. Pillar House, Troy VI
22. House VIf, Troy VI
23. House VIc, Troy VI
24. House VIe, Troy VI
25. House 731, Troy VII
26. Temple of Athena, Troy VIII–IX
27. *Propylon* of Athena sanctuary, Troy VIII–IX
28. Outer wall of Athena sanctuary, Troy VIII–IX
29. Inner wall of Athena sanctuary, Troy VIII–IX
30. Sanctuary of Demeter-Cybele, Troy VIII–IX
31. Waterworks, Troy VIII–IX
32. *Bouleuterion*, Troy IX
33. *Odeion*, Troy IX
34. Gymnasium-bath complex, Troy IX

Troy I
Troy II
Troy VI
Troy VII
Troy VIII–IX

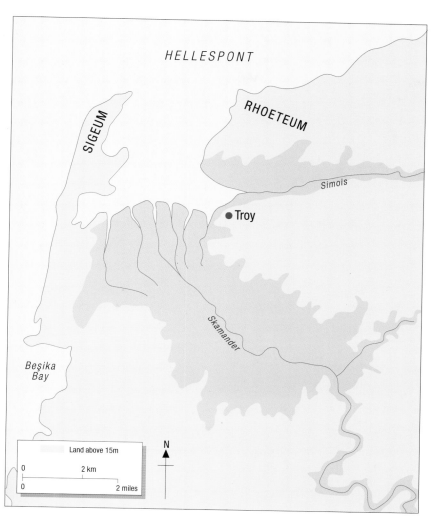

LEFT Troy and its surroundings in the Late Bronze Age, with the Dardanelles (Homer's Hellespont), the marine embayment, and the litoral plain. Also shown is Beşika Bay, the site of a possible Mycenaean cemetery.

BELOW Looking south-west towards the promontory at Beşika Bay. The conical mound on the left of the picture is the so-called Tomb of Achilles (Beşik Tepe), the scene of visits by Alexander the Great and Lord Byron. According to Plutarch, Alexander stripped naked and ran a ceremonial race round Achilles' grave mound. He says that Alexander also remarked that Achilles was most fortunate in having 'a great poet to sing of his deeds after his death' (*Alexander* 15.4). Byron also made a pilgrimage to the site, and then swum the Dardanelles from Abydos to Sestos in imitation of the ill-starred Leander. (Author's collection)

ABOVE Beşika Bay and the island of Tenedos (Bozcaada), looking south-west. In the legend of the Trojan War, the island plays a prominent part. On the way to Troy, Philoktetes, the leader of the seven ships from Methone, suffered a nasty snakebite when the Achaians landed at Tenedos to make a sacrifice. His pain was so great and his wound so unpleasant (especially the smell) that the army abandoned him against his will on the island, where he was left, literally, to rot. When the Achaians devised the strategy of the Wooden Horse filled with armed warriors and left in front of Troy, the army then withdrew to Tenedos, as if abandoning the war. (Author's collection)

RIGHT The sandy beach at Beşika Bay, looking north-east from the promontory. On the right of the picture is the 'Tomb of Achilles' (Beşik Tepe), nearby to which the cemetery was discovered. Excavated by Korfmann between 1982 and 1987, the graves contained imported Mycenaean goods together with material indigenous to the Troad, with pottery indicating a date on the borderline between Troy VIh and Troy VIIa, the traditional period of the Trojan War. (Author's collection)

straits from Asia to Europe. From its vantage grounds it could dominate traffic both across and up and down the narrow straits, and presumably tolls of some kind were extracted from those who passed by land or by sea. As a result, Troy gained wealth – and made enemies.

Still, the large bay in front of Troy must have been a magnet for Bronze Age seafarers, who had a safe haven once they had left the main channel of the Dardanelles. Opening directly onto the straits, the mouth of the bay between the rocky headlands of Sigeum (Kum Kale) and Rhoeteum (In Tepe) was about 2km across. Inside, it opened out to about 4km of shallow sea fringed by the alluvial flats of the rivers, salt marshes, reedy lagoons and wind-blown sand dunes. There would have been no real harbour, just a trading post where vessels tied up or, alternatively, simply put aground on the sandy shores. Unquestionably Troy had its own ships, not only for trading purposes but also war galleys to protect its maritime interests from perennial raiders and pirates. In turn, these oared warships would also have allowed the Trojans to raid for slaves and booty. Smaller, local craft would have included fishing-boats, especially at the time of the seasonal migrations of mackerel and tunny, which still swarm through the Dardanelles each autumn. The bay was also especially rich in shellfish, oysters and sea urchins.

To the south of Troy was perhaps a kilometre or two of alluvial plain stretching to the seashore. In the low-lying areas near to the Skamander much of the land was marshy in winter but otherwise dry. The alluvial soil, fertile enough where not waterlogged, could maintain a sizeable population. Barley was the chief food crop, although a small amount of domesticated emmer wheat, an old form of wheat first cultivated in Jericho (c. 9000 BC), was cultivated

in the drier margins. In and amongst the cereal stands would have been an abundance of arable weeds, which is still a typical feature of organically cultivated fields. Dotted amongst the latter were vineyards and olive groves, as well as stands of wild fig, pomegranate, tamarisk and cypress, whilst along the reedy banks of the meandering Skamander small oak, such as holm and valonia, would have been the predominate species.

With its abundance of small game, the water-margins of the Skamander served as a paradise for local hunters. Meanwhile, the higher areas of the undulating plain and along the limestone ridge provided pastureland, which allowed the Trojans to run mixed herds of cattle, sheep, goats, pigs and, with the foundation of Troy VI, domesticated horses. Up to this point Bronze Age Troy had been a thriving 'sheep town', exporting a fair percentage of its locally produced bales of wool, spun yarn and ready-made textiles further afield. Now horse breeding also featured as a major element in the Trojan economy, with both foals and fully grown horses being exported to the chariot kingdoms of the Near East.

Geography was to be Troy's greatest asset. On the one hand, Troy's particular geographical location was eminently suitable for agriculture, stockbreeding, fishing and hunting, thereby allowing its inhabitants to thrive. On the other hand, it also allowed its rulers to pursue with relative ease large-scale trade and to wield a geopolitical dominance over the vital land and sea routes between the East and the West. For a long time this strategic location would guarantee Troy its position as a wealthy commercial centre and a powerful political city. Power and profit, it is for these reasons that the same site, which was fortified from an early stage, would be continually settled for the duration of the Bronze Age.

The south curtain-wall of Troy I, looking west towards the well-preserved east bastion of the South Gate. Showing signs of having been repeatedly strengthened, the wall has a distinct batter and was constructed using unworked limestone blocks mortared together with clay. (Author's collection)

Troy I (c. 2900–2450 BC, Early Bronze Age II)

Built directly on bedrock, some 16m above sea level, the earliest settlement had a total of 11 building phases (Ia–Ik). It was an extremely small settlement, and even at the height of its development the diameter of Troy I was only 90m.

Despite its unpretentious size the settlement was always protected by well-planned fortifications. A circuit-wall of rough unworked stones, which was repeatedly improved and strengthened, encircled the citadel mound. This was pierced by two gateways that allowed access from the landward side. The south gateway (Gate FN), with its flanking four-cornered bastions, is one of the earliest fortified gateways in Anatolia. Still in a very good state of preservation, this impressive entranceway is 2.97m wide and shaped like a corridor. The extant remains of its east bastion reach to the height of 3.5m. The base of the bastion is composed of fairly large stones that become progressively smaller,

The south gateway (Gate FN) of Troy I, looking south from within the citadel. Complete with four-cornered bastions, this is one of the earliest gateways in Anatolia. (Author's collection)

the structure itself becoming distinctly narrower as it gains height. Any attack by an enemy trying to force the long corridor-like entrance would be parried from the flanking bastions. Adjoining the east bastion is a part of the circuit-wall, a wall that has a distinct batter (a receding slope of about 45 degrees) on its outer face and was solidly constructed using unworked limestone mortared together with clay. Estimated to have been some 2.5m thick near the top, there is evidence to show that a vertical parapet made of sun-dried mud-brick crowned this sloping wall.

In the 'Schliemann Trench' is a series of close-set long houses among which House 102 is conspicuous for its size (18.75m by 7m) and form. Both of its long walls extended in the front to create a porch. It had a hearth at the centre and another close to the eastern wall. The two platforms adjoining the long walls probably served as seats or beds. In the eastern corner a shallow pit was used for storing foodstuffs, and the bones of various animals and remains of shellfish discovered here prove that food was also eaten in this area. Two separate infant burials were discovered just beneath the floor, one an inhumation in a shallow pit covered by a flat stone, the other an internment in a broken ceramic urn. Four graves of the same kind were exposed in the open space immediately north of the house, and the six skeletons found have all proved to be newborn babies, proving the rate of infant mortality was relatively high in early Troy.

The walls of these houses were made of sun-dried mud-bricks containing straw and resting on a foundation of stones. The latter were laid in a herringbone style, that is the stones were set diagonally and then bound together by a thin clay mortar and plastered. Long, narrow apertures for light and ventilation were left in the upper parts of the walls near the roof. The floors were covered with beaten clay and polished, and woven mats were then laid on top. The flat roofs were made of horizontal wooden beams covered with reeds and copiously plastered with mud. There were probably openings in the roofs to allow the smoke to escape.

The lifestyle was based on agriculture, stockbreeding and fishing (cf. Homer's 'Hellespont where the fish swarm'), and also hunting to a lesser degree. Barley was the staple cereal crop, although emmer wheat makes its first appearance towards the end of this era. Pottery was handmade and monochrome grey or black. Spindle whorls, loom weights, and bone and copper needles of various sizes indicate that these people were familiar with weaving. Stone beads and ornaments, bone and stone idols, and the incised decoration encountered on baked clay pottery appear to have been their only contact with moulded art. The limestone relief of a human face found by Blegen is regarded as being the oldest example of sculpture encountered in the area so far. Weapons and tools were made from obsidian or flint or from raw copper or lead.

The Troy I culture has a distribution covering the coastal regions of the northern Aegean and the Sea of Marmara. Trade and cultural connections are attested far into the Mediterranean, Europe and Anatolia. Archaeologists believe that the history of Troy I ended with a fire.

Troy II (c. 2450–2200 BC, Early Bronze Age II)

Although Troy I was destroyed catastrophically, there was no break in the time sequence or any change in the culture between the two settlements. On the contrary, the culture of Troy I continued to develop in Troy II.

The seat of an important king or chieftain, the citadel of Troy II was solidly planned and strongly built on an area of no more than 9,000 m² (c. 0.9ha). To this citadel, however, there belonged a lower town, whose existence has been demonstrated in the recent excavations. After eight building phases (IIa–IIh) and many alterations to the fortification walls, it was twice destroyed by terrible conflagrations. With its precise plan, rarely encountered in other settlements of the period, the 'Burnt City' (Troy IIg) is one of the most impressive monuments

The south-west gateway (Gate FM) of Troy II, looking north-east. Leading up to the gateway is a steep, well-paved ramp with a parapet. At the point where the ramp and the entrance meet there stood a wooden door of two leaves strengthened with copper or bronze sheets. This gateway has four inner pilasters, two on each side, which narrowed the entrance at these two points, and is the earliest example of this type. (Author's collection)

of the Early Bronze Age. It was originally considered by Schliemann to be the Troy described by Homer. However, Schliemann learned more in the course of his excavations and he probably recognised his mistake, a mistake that today we can see to be of the magnitude of roughly 1,250 years.

A circuit-wall, some 330m long and 4m thick with a limestone substructure surmounted by a perpendicular superstructure of sun-dried mud-brick, encircled the citadel mound. Four small, rectangular towers, about 3.8m wide and projecting 2.25m beyond the circuit-wall, added to the defensive strength of the *enceinte* on its landward side. This was pierced by two monumental gateways that allowed access from the landward side via the lower town below.

The south-east and south-west gateways have typical entrance chambers, and leading up to the latter (Gate FM) is a steep, well-paved ramp (21 by 7.55m) with a stone parapet that once supported a mud-brick superstructure. The ramp rises some 5m to the level of the gateway at a gradient of approximately one in four, too steep for wheeled traffic. At the point where the ramp and the 5.25m-wide entrance meet there once stood a double-rung wooden door, which was strengthened with copper or bronze sheets. This gateway has four inner pilasters, two on each side, which purposely narrows the entrance at these two points, and is the earliest example of this type. The south-east gateway (Gate FO), though of greater dimensions, exhibits essentially the same plan as the south-west gateway, except that no ramp was built as the ground here falls off in a gentle slope toward the plateau occupied by the lower town.

A further gateway (*Propylon* IIc) and a roofed colonnade separated off the interior of the citadel. Within lie the remains of large long houses with porches, the so-called megaron-style of building. The most common feature of the megaron was the existence of a hearth situated in the centre of the room. Particularly noteworthy is the huge size (35m by 13m) of the largest of the megaron buildings (Megaron IIA), and the long period of its use. It had two floors and probably served as an assembly room or an audience-hall, although the recent finds of cult amphora with idols in adoration gestures on the handles suggest that in its last phase (IIh) it was a place of cultic activity.

From in and on the burnt debris of the citadel came the more than 20 'Troy Treasures', including the legendary 'Priam's Treasure' (cf. Homer's 'Troy rich in gold'). These treasures – jewellery and drinking vessels of gold, silver, electrum, bronze and copper – demonstrate that Troy II had extensive trading links reaching out in all directions of the compass. In particular, the jewellery are masterpieces of craftsmanship (granulation and filigree work, as well as enamelling) such as are rarely found outside Mesopotamia and Egypt during this period. The settlement obviously had very skilful metalworkers that presumably offered their services to foreign rulers, travelling from one region to another. Among the metals they worked are gold, silver, lead and copper – all found in Anatolia – and tin, which is thought to have been imported from the Zagros Mountains (southern Iran) or the Iberian Peninsula.

Amongst the more mundane finds, pounding or grinding stones and decorated spindle whorls are numerous. The high number of sheep and goat bones confirms the expanding yarn and weaving industry. The inhabitants probably utilised metal scissors to shear sheep and did not have to pluck them by hand as their Mesopotamia counterparts did. Beans, lentils or vetch and emmer wheat are known to have been added to the already existing food sources such as domestic animals and seafood. Most unusual in these latitudes is the extensive use of the potter's wheel. Likewise the possession of bronze, an alloy of copper and tin, a crucial prerequisite for the mass production of cast metal weapons and therefore for military superiority. However, archaeologists believe that Troy II suddenly succumbed to attack. The layer of destruction that represents the end of Troy IIg is on average 1m thick and bears all the hallmarks of a deliberate holocaust.

Troy III–V (c. 2200–1700 BC, Early Bronze Age III to Middle Bronze Age)

The foreign invaders who destroyed Troy II did not occupy the site, since no evidence has been found of a change in culture during the subsequent settlements of Troy III–V. During this era, however, what we do witness is the gradual fading of the former glory of Troy and its decline in prosperity.

Over the centuries the citadel expanded to cover an area of 18,000m^2 (c. 1.8ha), but there is no evidence to indicate that the lower town continued to flourish. Schliemann at the beginning of his investigations mainly excavated the settlements of Troy III–V. But his sequence has now been further subdivided on the basis of the excavations of Blegen into four building phases in Troy III (IIIa–IIId), five in Troy IV (IVa–IVe), and four in Troy V (Va–Vd). In the light of his own excavations, Korfmann now considers Troy I–III as one cultural unit, the 'Maritime Troia Culture'.

Although each seems to have had a circuit-wall, it has been assumed that the settlements of Troy III–V were rather impoverished, with small houses standing contiguously, one beside another, and narrow, winding streets. Yet some of the artefacts that make up 'Priam's Treasure' may derive from these strata. The domed oven makes its first appearance on the site during this period. Hunting provides a markedly greater proportion of the diet, with venison as the most popular kind of meat. The rather abrupt appearance of deer in appreciably greater numbers than before presumably mean that new methods of hunting had been developed, such as the acquisition of better deer hounds or the invention of more effective weapons of the hunt. There is little change, however, in the pottery. Typical pots and tall slender, two-handled goblets (cf. Homer's *depas amphikypellon* for wine). The final building-phase (Vd) was destroyed by fire.

Troy VI (c. 1700–1250 BC, Middle Bronze Age to Late Bronze Age)

A completely new princely or royal citadel was built covering an area of 20,000m^2 (c. 2ha). In size, and probably in importance, it surpassed the citadel previously known at Hisarlik and all others so far investigated in western Anatolia. Eight building phases (VIa–VIh) and three main periods (Early, Middle, Late) can be identified which represent the long, continuous history of the site, from the opening of the Middle Helladic period to the Late Helladic III

Troy VI, the 'guardian of the Hellespont'

A reconstructed panoramic view, of Troy VI looking west. Of note is the seascape – especially the marine embayment and the mouth of the Dardanelles – thereby emphasising Troy's intimate relationship with the sea. The city not only controlled the Straits, but also had a thriving wool industry and traded throughout the eastern Mediterranean, Near East and Central Asia. Away from the embayment and on the landward side of Troy and nearby its walls was pasturage, with relatively large flocks of sheep and herds of goats, interspersed with small plots of arable land. Here and there were vineyards, olive groves and cypress stands.

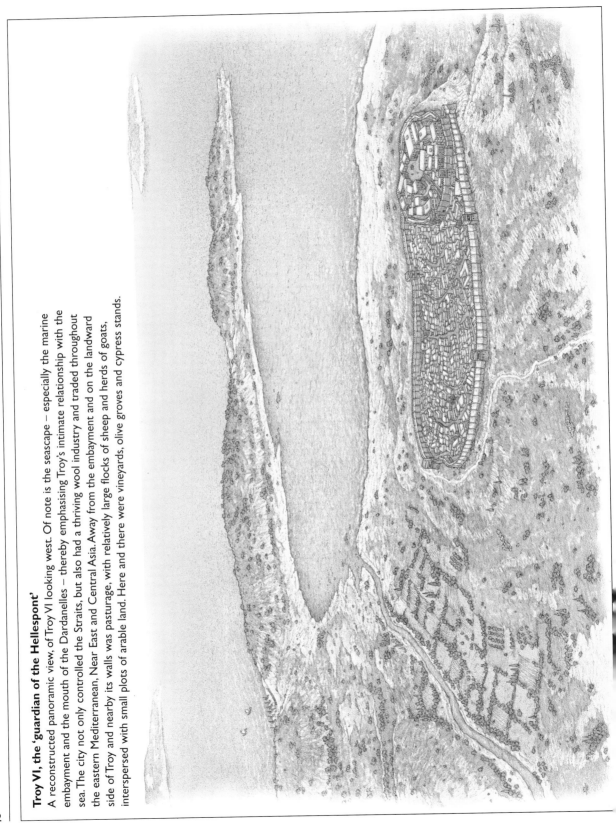

period on the Greek mainland and the Hittite New Kingdom period in central Anatolia.

The fortifications around the citadel are in a new style, amounting to some 550m in length and technically superior, consisting of gently sloping walls of well-cut masonry with vertical offsets and massive towers (cf. Homer's 'angle of the lofty walls', and 'strong-towered Ilios'). The circuit-wall, which can still be seen today, is 4 to 5m thick and more than 6m high, it would have reached up a further 3 to 4m with its vertical mud-brick superstructure. Five gateways and posterns led into the citadel, with the principal gateway (Gate VIT) lying to the south flanked by a tower (Tower VIi) notable for the six monolithic stelae that stood along its front (cf. Homer's 'Skaian Gate'). From this gateway a wide paved street (Street 710), complete with a central drain, led up into the heart of the citadel.

Behind the fortifications, buildings in the interior were disposed on three concentric terraces rising up towards the centre of the citadel mound. There were palatial free-standing buildings, including megara, sometimes two-storied and invariably trapezoidal in plan, with their shorter sides facing the summit and their longer sides facing the fortifications. Of importance are House VIE, with its steep retaining wall of smooth-cut stones, and House VIF with its stone supports and its recesses for stout wooden beams, while on the floor are 12 stone bases for pillars. Equally interesting is the once two-storied House VIM with its L-shaped plan and its carefully built retaining wall, nearly 27m long, which once had a smoothly finished sloping outer face that was marked off by four vertical offsets into five segments. Even in decay the building displays a very attractive silhouette, rising up in the form of a miniature fortress. It is assumed that the royal residence lay on the summit, and House VIM surely formed part of the Troy VI palace complex. Most of its remains were removed when the temple of Athena was rebuilt in the early 3rd century BC (Troy VIII). The whole imposing layout of the citadel, undoubtedly planned by a central authority, was excavated under Dörpfeld's direction and he rightly interpreted it to be Homer's Troy.

The final building phase (VIh) was severely damaged by an earthquake, as is evident from the large vertical cracks in the surviving fortification walls.

General view of the plain of Simois looking north-west from the north-east bastion (Tower VIG) towards the islands of Imbros (Gokceada) and Samothraki. Today local farmers exploit this silted plain for its valuable cotton crop, but in the time of Troy VI it would have been part of the marine embayment.
According to Homer, 'aloft on top of the highest summit of timbered Samothraki' Poseidon gazed upon the fighting on the plain of Troy (*Iliad* 13.12). Indeed, if you climb Mount Fengári (1,560m) the view from its peak is all embracing, with the plain of Troy and Mount Ida in the far distance to the east. (Author's collection)

The truly splendid extant remains of the east fortification-walls of the citadel of Troy VI, looking north. The fortifications were constructed using closely fitted limestone blocks, so finely jointed that no mortar was used, and surmounted by a timber-framed superstructure of mud-brick and plaster. In the foreground stands the east tower (Tower VIH), which covers the approach to the east gateway (Gate VIs). Between the two runs the east curtain-wall with its distinctive batter. (Author's collection)

Nevertheless, Dörpfeld found evidence for fire or fires at various places in the destruction level of Troy VIh and saw this destruction as the work of men. Likewise Korfmann's excavation has also revealed signs of war, namely a thick charcoal layer dated roughly to 1250 BC, as well as slingshots, bronze spearheads and arrowheads scattered in the debris and lodged in the fortification walls. Of course, linking Hisarlik to Homer will always prove to be highly controversial.

In 1988 Korfmann began a renewed attempt to find a lower town to the citadel of Troy VI. Its existence has since been demonstrated and it is now known that it was bordered by a defensive installation some 450m to the south of the citadel mound. 'Negative' signs of impressive wooden structures have also been revealed and these are believed to be the houses that once crowded the lower town. With a settlement covering an area of nearly 270,000m² (c. 27ha), Troy VI is now 13 times larger than previously supposed. Its population has been estimated at between 5,000 to 10,000 inhabitants. These findings place Troy among the larger trading and palatial settlements of Anatolia and the Near East in this period.

Completely new styles of pottery imitate metal prototypes. This is particularly the case with grey luxury-ware, referred to as Grey Minyan Ware, which is burnished and decorated mostly with horizontal wavy lines. This type of pottery has a distribution as far afield as mainland Greece. Indeed, there are intensive commercial and cultural links with the Aegean and the Mycenaean world that are documented by an orderly sequence of imported Mycenaean ware found in the eight strata (VIa–VIh) with increasing regularity as time goes by. Another notable innovation was the frequent use of the horse, attested by a skeleton and finds of numerous other equine bones (cf. Homer's 'horse-taming Trojans', or 'Ilios, famed for its horses'). Likewise, several pommels of white marble or of alabaster, found from throughout the history of Troy VI, offer evidence that the sword was no longer a rare commodity. This conclusion is supported by the discovery of numerous whetstones of a new type. These are pencil-like hones clearly designed to facilitate the sharpening of blades to a keen edge.

It can be concluded that the inhabitants of Troy VI were people of a different culture to those of the previous settlements. This new stock of vigorous people employed horse-drawn chariots in war, utilised efficient bronze weapons and also built strong fortifications that display increased knowledge of military engineering together with technical advances in masonry. It has been suggested that the earliest chariot warfare took place in Anatolia and chariot-warriors may have established Troy VI (Drews 1993: 106). Arriving in Troy with this new military technology, the Neo-Trojans soon came to dominate the Troad.

Troy VII (c. 1250–1050 BC, Late Bronze Age to Early Iron Age)

The remains of houses of Troy VI, together with parts of the citadel fortifications, were hastily repaired and reused and many new ones built in former empty spaces. There is no cultural break between Troy VIh and Troy VIIa but, from the point of view of workmanship, a considerable drop in quality. For the new domestic structures are noticeably shabbier, smaller and more cramped, while the rebuilt houses are partitioned. All the evidence points to an increase in population, and in the number of large storage-vessels (*pithoi*) set deeply into the ground, inside the citadel.

A close-up view of the east curtain-wall of Troy VI, looking north from the east tower (Tower VIH) towards the east gateway (Gate VIs). The walls of Troy VI are characterised by vertical offsets of 10 to 15cm at about every 10m, thereby breaking the circuit-wall up into sections. This is a novel feature of Trojan fortification architecture, which is functional rather than decorative, and distinguishes it from Mycenaean and Hittite work. As clearly seen here, these offsets show slight changes of direction in the curtain-wall, thus allowing it to turn without the use of corners, the weak points in any defensive system. (Author's collection)

Some have attributed this phenomenon to the fact that the Trojans of this period did not feel secure and thus had adopted a 'siege mentality'. Whereas Dörpfeld's view (1902: 181-2) had been that the city destroyed by Homer's Achaians (*Achaiwoí*) was Troy VIh, Blegen (1953: 14, 331) equated the Troy VIIa settlement, which he believed was captured, looted and put to the torch, with Homer's Troy. Blegen's arguments remain influential. However, considerations of the architecture and planning of Troy VIIa make it difficult to share this orthodoxy. For although the inhabitants repaired the fortifications and the ruined houses, they did not achieve the high artistic standards and intricately thought-out town planning representative of Troy VIh.

The subsequent building-phases (VIIb$_1$–VIIb$_2$) show considerable continuity, with, for example, parts of the fortification walls remaining in use. Yet there are significant new cultural elements, such as crude handmade pottery suddenly reappearing after the potter's wheel had been used for centuries. There are also changes in wall-building techniques, with the lower parts of the circuit-wall now being faced with irregular, vertically placed stone slabs (orthostats).

How Troy VIIb$_1$ perished is unclear. There is no evidence of destruction whether by earthquake or by human hands and probably the settlement was taken over by a related cultural group without serious disturbance. Prominent amongst the handmade pottery is a striking dark-coloured ware decorated *inter alia* with ribs and knobs like horns, the so-called Knobbed Ware or *Buckelkeramik*, for which analogies are to be found in south-eastern Europe. Similarly, a number of bronze axe heads found by Schliemann, although their context of discovery is not certain, have been attributed to Troy VIIb$_2$ and have

Three megaron-type houses of Troy VI/VII, House VIE (right, front), House VIC (right, rear), and House VIF (left) looking west. Situated on one of the terraces below the palace complex, these once impressive two-storeyed buildings would have belonged to the retainers and kinsmen of the royal family. The rectangular cuttings in the west internal wall of House VIF once held wooden support beams, while the upper storey was wood-framed with mud-brick and plaster. The remains of the east gateway (Gate VIs) run in the foreground of the picture. (Author's collection)

their best parallels in Late Bronze Age Hungary. As the *Buckelkeramik* has a parallel across the Hellespont it appears that its makers may have migrated into the Troad from Thrace, to which in turn they may have moved from further west. Troy VIIb$_2$ was brought to an end by fire. Conceivably the settlement was taken by force and put to the torch.

Troy VIII (c. 700–85 BC, Archaic to Hellenistic Periods)

According to current scholarly opinion some 250 years later, at the time when Homer lived, Aeolian Greeks from the north-western Aegean resettled the mostly abandoned site. Remains of Troy VI/VII monuments were incorporated in the newly erected fortification walls and houses.

At first it was a modest settlement, although literary sources do mention a temple of Athena of this period despite its notable absence in the archaeological record. Herodotos, for example, says that Xerxes, prior to crossing the Hellespont

General view, looking west, of the sanctuary (possibly dedicated to Cybele-Demeter) of Troy VIII/IX, which was a prominent feature of Greek Ilion and Roman Ilium and just to the south-west of the Late Bronze Age citadel. Clearly visible are a number of altars and sacrificial pits. The high altar at the centre is assumed to have been built initially towards the end of the 4th century BC, while its marble steps and revetments are Roman. On the far right runs the north wall of the sanctuary, which stands immediately in front of the citadel wall of Troy VI. (Author's collection)

en route to conquer Greece, 'sacrificed a thousand oxen to the Trojan Athena' (7.43). Almost 150 years later and having crossed the Hellespont in the opposite direction, Alexander the Great also made a pilgrimage to Troy. He went to the temple of Athena and, in the words of Arrian, 'dedicated his full armour in the temple, and took down in its place some of the dedicated arms yet remaining from the Trojan War' (*Anabasis* 1.11.7).

Later, and especially in the time of Lysimachos, one of Alexander the Great's successors, there was deliberate veneration of the 'sacred city of Ilion', with the building of a sanctuary dedicated to Cybele-Demeter outside to the south-west and the rebuilding of the temple to Athena on the citadel mound. Of the

latter, nothing remains apart from a few blocks from the superstructures of the altars and some scattered marble components. When the temple was rebuilt, if not before, the central and most elevated buildings of Troy VI and Troy VII were cut away. To the south a lower town of regular design extended over and among the ruins of the lower town of Troy VI/VII.

In 85 BC, during the war against Mithridates VI Eupator, the site was thoroughly destroyed by the renegade Roman legate C. Flavius Fimbria. It is said he afterwards boasted that he had done in 11 days what the Achaians took ten years to accomplish. One Trojan wit responded by saying that they had not had Hector to defend the city.

Troy IX (48 BC–AD 550, Roman Period)

C. Iulius Caesar rebuilt Troy after a visit to the site in 48 BC. Indeed, the Romans had a very particular interest in Troy, tracing their ancestry back to the Trojan hero Aeneas, son of Aphrodite (Venus). According to post-Homeric legend, Aeneas not only survived the sack of Troy but also fled to Latium in Italy. As a result, the Romans viewed the Trojan hero as their progenitor and believed Troy to be the 'mother-city' of Rome. This belief is well documented on coins of Caesar, whose clan, the *gens Iulia*, developed their political ideology by claiming Iulus (Ascanius), son of Aeneas, as eponymous founder and thus descent from his divine grandmother Venus. A noteworthy example is the silver *denarius* of Caesar portraying the flight of Aeneas with the Palladium, a small wooden image of armed Athena, in his right hand and his father Anchises on his back.

Troy's chief landmark was the Doric temple of Athena, and this was rebuilt and enlarged, especially under Caesar's heir and successor Augustus (r. 27 BC–AD 14). Of this monument there survive only the long sections of the massive foundations supporting the porticoes and surrounding walls of the 9,500 m² rectangular sacred precinct. On the southern slope of the ruins of 'sacred Ilium', as the Romans called Troy, are altars and a *bouleuterion* (council-chamber), also an *odeion*, which, among other things, was intended for the presentation of musical performances. These two public buildings date from the period of Augustus but were extensively rebuilt under Hadrian (r. AD 117–38). Not far from these civic buildings is a gymnasium-bath complex with mosaic floors. North-east of the temple platform is a large theatre set into a natural declivity that offers a view of the Simois valley and the Dardanelles beyond. Although only partially excavated, it is claimed that the theatre could have held over 6,000 spectators.

Scattered marble architectural elements are all that remain of the Temple of Athena, once a dominant feature of Troy VIII/IX. Probably built by Lysimachos, one of Alexander the Great's successors, around 300 BC and restored by order of the Emperor Augustus (r. 27 BC–AD 14) whose imperial family, the Iulio-Claudians, honoured Troy ('Sacred Ilium') as the supposed home of their ancestor Aeneas, whose mother was the goddess Venus. Visible in the background are the ruins of the foundation wall of the temple precinct, which covered an area of some 9,500m². The precinct was the focal point of a great annual festival in honour of Athena, which was marked with sacrifices and athletic contests. (Author's collection)

The ruins of the public gymnasium-bath complex of Troy IX, looking south. Here mosaic floors were discovered (no longer preserved) decorated with human and animal figures. In the same location, archaeologists discovered a burial ground, which is thought to have been used during the last period of Troy VI. Cremated human remains had been placed in *pithoi*, which were covered with a stone lid and stood upright often just a few centimetres below the ground. (Author's collection)

Ilium received generous patronage from the emperors until the 3rd century AD. The lower town was rebuilt and several times enlarged following the traditional Roman *insula* system, that is, the gridiron pattern. Ilium received its water supply from the foothills of Mount Ida by means of aqueducts and clay pipes. Constantine the Great (r. AD 324–37) at first planned to build his new capital at Ilium and construction work was even begun before that at Constantinople (Istanbul).

Under Constantine Christianity became an officially recognised religion, and Ilium became the seat of a bishopric. Interestingly, Iulian the Apostate (r. AD 361–63) relates in a letter that when he visited he found that at the Episcopal See of Ilium there were still fires burning on the altars and that the cult statue of Hector was still anointed with sacred oil. The 'Tomb of Achilles' was also intact. Iulian, an ardent Hellenist who worshipped the 'old gods', soon realised that it was the local 'Bishop of the Galilaeans' himself who was keeping the flame burning (*Epistle* 19). Despite its sanctity, however, the once proud municipality appears to have entered a period of gradual decline, perhaps because of the loss of its economic significance through the silting of its harbour. Eventually it was abandoned, but not forgotten.

The Roman *odeion* of Troy IX, looking north-east. Serving as a public meeting place and concert-hall, this civic building was renovated by order of the Emperor Hadrian (r. AD 117–38). The *odeion* has a semicircular orchestra, with a stage building (*skene*) in which stood a larger-than-life cuirassed statue of Hadrian. Behind the orchestra are the rising tiers of seats constructed out of large limestone blocks and divided by aisles into wedge-shaped sections. Immediately behind the *odeion* itself runs the south curtain-wall of Troy VI, and visible is a pillar belonging to the 'Pillar House', one of the largest houses in Troy VI. (Author's collection)

Mud-brick construction

efore we turn our attention to the fortifications of Troy VI, a word or two on mud-brick construction is necessary. What may seem a digression at first glance will become a matter of relevance when it is considered that mud-brick was the common building material of Troy. Moreover, the Trojans who made their houses of mud-brick did not use the material solely for this purpose, for the fortification walls that protected them were also, in part, constructed of mud-brick.

Mud-brick as a building material, both for civic and military architecture, has a long history that stretches back into early Near Eastern practice, where it is still carried on – in a domestic role at least – using age-old techniques. The method of making or 'striking' bricks used today by the Egyptian brickmaker is, therefore, worth description.

Modern Egypt

First, the brickmaker searches for a deposit of Nile mud of a suitable consistency for his purpose and clears as large and flat a space as possible. His assistant, the mud-mixer, then digs up the mud and puts it into a smallish hole in the ground, where water is slowly added to it until it has the consistency of a very thick homogenous paste. The mixing is done with the aid of a cultivator's hoe, the feet assisting in the operation. During this part of the process sand and chopped straw are mixed in varying amounts with the mud paste. Having thoroughly mixed up the paste, the mud-mixer then takes a

The fresco from the tomb of Rekhmira, once vizier of Upper Egypt during the reigns of Thutmose III and Amenhetep II (1479–1401 BC), showing the various stages involved in the manufacture of mud-bricks. Scene one depicts two men taking Nile mud from a pool. Scene two has them working the material into a homogenous paste. Scene three shows the brick paste being compressed into individual wooden moulds, the work being directed by an overseer armed with a switch. In scene four the bricks are being stacked so as to dry them in the sun. Finally, in scene five the finished bricks are being laid in order to construct a wall. (Reproduced from Gardner Wilkinson, J, *The Ancient Egyptians: Their Life and Customs*, John Murray, London, 1854)

round mat made of strips of palm leaf and, having dusted it over with fine dry mud to prevent sticking, he puts as much of the paste on it as he can carry and leaves it beside the brickmaker.

The brickmaker squats down holding an oblong wooden mould fitted with a handle, the mould being the size of the bricks he wishes to strike. Having filled the mould with the mud paste, the brickmaker scrapes off the surplus and lifts the mould, leaving a sticky mud-brick just sufficiently hard to retain its form. He continues striking a series of such bricks, one alongside the other but slightly apart, until the available space is filled. The bricks are left to dry in the sun for about three days before being turned over and, by the end of a week they are firm enough to be stacked up in a pattern that allows the air to circulate. A week or two latter they appear quite dry, though they may be damp inside, and are now ready for building. Brick walls are built without scaffolding; the builders simply walk on top of the section they have built. Since they are barefooted their weight helps to solidify the work.

Ancient Egypt

In ancient Egypt the method was identical with that used today, the only difference being that in the Egyptian frescoes we see the mud paste being carried in a pot instead of on a mat. A New Kingdom fresco from the tomb of Rekhmira, once vizier of Upper Egypt during the reigns of Thutmose III and Amenhetep II (1479–1401 BC), shows the various stages involved in the manufacture of mud-bricks. Scene one depicts two men taking Nile mud from a pool. Scene two has them working the material into a paste. In scene three the brick paste is being compressed into individual wooden moulds, the work being directed by an overseer armed with a switch. Scene four shows the bricks being stacked so as to dry in the sun. Finally, in scene five we witness the finished bricks being laid in order to construct a wall. The ancient bricklayers worked very much as do their modern counterparts, except that, instead of cement mortar, they laid in mud identical to that with which the bricks were made. Before the mud mortar dried, it united with the adjoining bricks, so that all cohered as a unity.

Mud and straw

Accompanying the fresco from the tomb of Rekhmira is an inscription that reads 'making bricks to build anew the storehouse of the temple of Karnak' (Spencer 1979: 3). Of all the surviving monuments of Egypt, the most famous are the great stone pyramids of Giza and the stone-built mortuary temples of Luxor and Abydos. However, the vast majority of Egyptian buildings were constructed more rapidly and economically by the extensive use of sun-dried mud-brick as the major material. Herodotos (2.136), for instance, mentions the brick pyramid of Asychis (Sheshonq I, founder of the XXII Dynasty) on which the following inscription can be read:

Do not consider me mean in comparison with stone pyramids, for I am as far above them as Zeus above the other gods. For they thrust a pole deep into a marsh and collected that which

Today, a practised Egyptian brickmaker with one assistant can shape as many as 1,500 bricks in a day. The bricks are left to dry in the sun for about three days before being turned over, and by the end of a week they are firm enough to be stacked up in a pattern that allows the air to circulate. A week or two latter they appear quite dry, though they may be damp inside, and are now ready for building. Brick walls are built without scaffolding; the builders simply walk on top of the section they have built. Since they are barefooted their weight helps to solidify the work.
(Author's collection)

remained of the mud on the pole, and made bricks therefrom. In this way they have built me.

Alternatively, the Babylonians, again according to Herodotos (*fl.* 450 BC), fashioned bricks for their city wall 'out of the earth which was thrown out of the fosse' (1.179). Similarly, though on a much smaller scale, in 429 BC the Peloponnesians, having failed with their siege mound and siege engines, decided to invest Plataia by encircling it with a mud-brick wall. The clay for the bricks, according to the contemporary Athenian historian Thucydides (2.78.1), came from the ditches they dug both inside and outside the line of circumvallation.

Modern studies show that pure Nile mud may shrink by over 30 per cent in drying, but the sand and straw serve to make the brick dry and shrink as one unit, thereby preventing the formation of cracks. Although their frescoes do not necessarily depict this part of the manufacturing process, the ancient Egyptians clearly understood the problem caused by shrinkage and the means to overcome it. The Old Testament (*Exodus* 5:7) mentions the manufacture of bricks in Egypt by Hebrew slaves, and it is stated that straw was used in the process. The sun-dried bricks of El-Kâb and those of the Dahshûr pyramids contained, beside chopped straw, calf's hair, animal dung, plant leaves and parts of grasses. The use of straw or other organic substances raises the tensile strength of the bricks. Again modern studies confirm that straw alone will raise the breaking strength of a brick by 244 per cent, while the addition of manure produces an exceptionally hard brick.

In many parts of modern Egypt houses are still primarily built from sun-dried mud-brick. Cheap, and in plentiful supply, mud-bricks are formed by hand, generally using a rectangular wooden mould. Once dry the bricks are surprisingly durable. To make bricks, Nile mud is mixed with sand, straw and water, packed down into wooden moulds and then slapped out onto the ground to dry in the full sun. This process has not changed much since people began to settle in the Nile valley. (Author's collection)

31

The siege of Mantineia

When Pausanias (8.8.7–8) makes reference to the siege of Mantineia, that mounted by Agesipolis of Sparta in 385 BC, he says the following:

Against the blows of engines brick brings greater security than fortifications built of stone. For stones break and are dislodged from their fittings; brick however, does not suffer so much from engines, but it crumbles under the action of water just as wax is melted by the sun.

Agesipolis' siege of Mantineia ideally illustrates the inherent problem of employing mud-brick fortifications, that is, their vulnerability to water. After initially laying waste to the surrounding countryside, says Xenophon (*Hellenika* 5.2.4), the Spartan commander detailed half of his army to dig a trench and erect a siege-wall around the city, thereby investing it. Despite this, however, the Mantineians continued to hold out as they had taken the precaution of stockpiling a large reserve of grain within their walls. Not wishing to commit the forces of his Peloponnesian allies to a long and drawn-out siege, Agesipolis resorted to the stratagem of diverting the river Ophis, which flowed through the city, by use of a makeshift dam. Due to the heavy rains of the previous winter the river was in full spate and, subsequently, the diverted water soon rose above the stone plinth of the circuit-wall. As the rising water began to melt the lower courses of mud-brick, the upper ones also weakened. First cracks begun to appear in the wall's superstructure and then signs of collapse. Even though the Mantineians valiantly shored up their crumbling defences with timber, total collapse was imminent, and so it was decided that the best course of action was to surrender (Xenophon *Hellenika* 5.2.4–5, cf. Diodoros 15.12.1).

M. Vitruvius Pollio, the military-engineer who served C. Iulius Caesar describes in detail the properties that a good brick should have and also the forms in which it is best prepared. He says (2.3.1) that the clay used for making bricks should be neither sandy nor stony nor gritty. It should be capable of being kneaded easily. The best materials are white chalky clay, red earth or 'male', a very firm and hard sand. The bricks made from either one of these materials are light and at the same time solid. In the State of California, where sun-dried mud-brick (adobe) is still used for domestic architecture, the 1991 Uniform Building Code (Section 24-15, 2403) specifies the clay content of the bricks must be between 25 and 45 per cent. Too much clay and the brick cracks as it dries and too little clay means the brick will be weak and crumbly when it dries. Care must be taken that the outer layer does not dry up while the interior is still wet. If wet bricks are used for building they contract in the wall and they work themselves loose from the plaster, which then falls off. Vitruvius (2.3.2) recommends drying for two years in the shade, beginning in spring or autumn rather than in the heat of summer, for then drying out will take place slowly and uniformly.

Taking precautions

An unprotected mud-brick edifice would have had a very limited life span and the chance that the whole structure might revert to mud necessitated precautions at every level. A stone plinth obviated the worst menace, that of contact with standing water, its height varying according to the terrain traversed by the circuit-wall and the climatic conditions indigenous to the locality. Upon completion, the whole surface of the mud-brick superstructure was smoothed with mud and plastered with clay or lime to prevent rainwater percolating into the joints. The plastering of mud-brick fortifications is well attested in late 4th-century BC Athenian inscriptions (*IG* II² 167.82–84, 463.81–85, 106–9, 1663, 1664). Likewise, Thucydides (3.20.3) mentions that the unplastered sections on the face of the Peloponnesian siege-wall at Plataia revealed the brickwork beneath.

Walls coated with pure clay were more attractive and durable, with a perfectly smooth surface having a hardness that is comparable to that of stone. The advantages of a clay over lime facing were considerable since, being subject to the same rate of contraction and expansion as the wall itself, the clay had less tendency to crack and peel. The one plus point in favour of a lime plaster was its ability to extract any extraneous water from a new wall. Another requirement was to prevent rainwater from collecting along the top of the wall, especially around the base of the battlements, which might be dangerously weakened. According to Thucydides' testimony (3.22.4) the battlements of Greek fortification walls were usually covered in terracotta tiles. However, if the wall carried a walkway (*parodos*) a more expensive paving of stone slabs was preferable to tiles. An Athenian inscription of 307/6 BC ordains that the *parodos* and other portions subjected to wear be given a hard covering imposed on a 'finger-thickness of sieved earth' (*IG* II² 463.81–85).

The Egyptians habitually safeguarded their great structures of brickwork by laying it within a continuous skeleton of timber, the Middle Kingdom fortresses in Upper Nubia, for example, were all in mud-brick with timber bonding. An Athenian document of 307/6 BC orders repair of decayed brick walling to include binding with wooden baulks (*IG* II² 463.74–75) and it figured in a makeshift addition to the circuit-wall of Plataia, thereby 'preventing the structure from becoming weak as it attained height' (Thucydides 2.75.4-5).

Pros and cons

Completion in brick unquestionably saved a great deal of time and money as bricks could be made rapidly with little apparatus and by unskilled labour. In the extant texts dealing with his fifth campaign the Assyrian king Sennacherib

Mud-brick house, Assiros, Macedonia. This method of construction has many advantages; it is fast and easy, repairs can be easily undertaken and additions or changes to a house can be done rapidly. Although of a domestic structure, this image does show the fundamental characteristics of all mud-brick edifices, such as the structure that topped Troy's *enceinte*. The stone plinth obviates the menace of contact with standing water, while the over-hanging terracotta tiles prevent rainwater from collecting along the top of the wall. Upon completion, as was the case with Troy, the whole surface of the mud-brick superstructure can then be smoothed with mud and plastered with clay or lime to prevent rainwater from percolating into the joints. (Author's collection)

r. 704–681 BC) proudly boasts that he enslaved all those who did not submit to his will and promptly forced them 'to carry the headpan and mould bricks' Luckenbill 1968: 166.383). Nor were speed and cheapness the only advantages brick offered. Mud-brick is fireproof and practically indestructible to the weather when the surface is properly protected. It also has considerable resiliency to minor earthquakes. Demosthenes of Athens speaks (3.25–26, 23.207) of the mud-brick houses of Themistokles, Miltiades and Aristides as still inhabited in his day, nearly 150 years later. Indeed they were evidently in good condition and quite indistinguishable from their neighbours.

According to Apollodoros of Damascus (*Poliorketika* 157.1–158.3), the Greek military engineer employed by both Trajan and Hadrian, and to Pausanias (8.8.7–8) a mud-brick fortification wall had a greater ability to resist a battering ram or the stone-shot from a catapult. Here the shock of impact was cushioned and localised, whereas in stone it was transmitted from block to block. On the other hand, if enemy sappers managed to reach the base of the brickwork they could easily cut a breach in a matter of minutes. Egyptian and Assyrian siege scenes often include sappers who, armed with rods and picks, are busy opening breaches in mud-brick ramparts (e.g. Nimrud, NW Palace Throne Room [British Museum 124552, 124553]).

Fortifications of Troy VI

The extant remains of the principal gateway (Gate VIт) lying to the south of the citadel of Troy VI, looking north. Clearly visible are the remains of the projecting tower (Tower VIı) that flanked the gateway, and in front of it the six stone stelae on which Dörpfeld thought images of the Trojan gods had been placed (cf. Homer's 'Skaian Gate'). In the centre of the picture can be seen the wide paved street, complete with a central drain, that led from the south gateway and ascended the terraces into th heart of the royal citadel. (Author's collection)

The fortifications of Troy VI are by no means of uniform style throughout and at least three major phases of the circuit-wall construction around the citadel mound are represented, which are hypothetically correlated with the Early Middle, and Late phases identified within the culture of Troy VI as a whole Corroborative evidence can be seen on the south side of the circuit-wall, where three successive gateways (Gates VIz, VIy, VIт) correspond to these three principa phases of fortification architecture. Gates VIy and VIz lie inside of VIт, just to th east of the so-called Pillar House, one of the largest houses in Troy VI.

Building programmes

The extant ruins of Troy VI give the impression that the citadel was divided radially into six sections (Sections 1–6) by wide streets starting from the five gateways (Gates VIR, VIs, VIz/y/т, VIu, VIv). The order of construction of the circuit-wall of Late Troy VI can thus be determined as follows. First Section 5 ir the west. Second, Sections 2 and 3 in the east, which are dated to Troy VIf Sections 1, 4, and 6 at the north-east, south, and north-west respectively, the las being securely dated to Troy VIg. Finally, the addition of the east and south towers (Towers VIн, VIı), which are both dated to the final building phase (VIh)

34

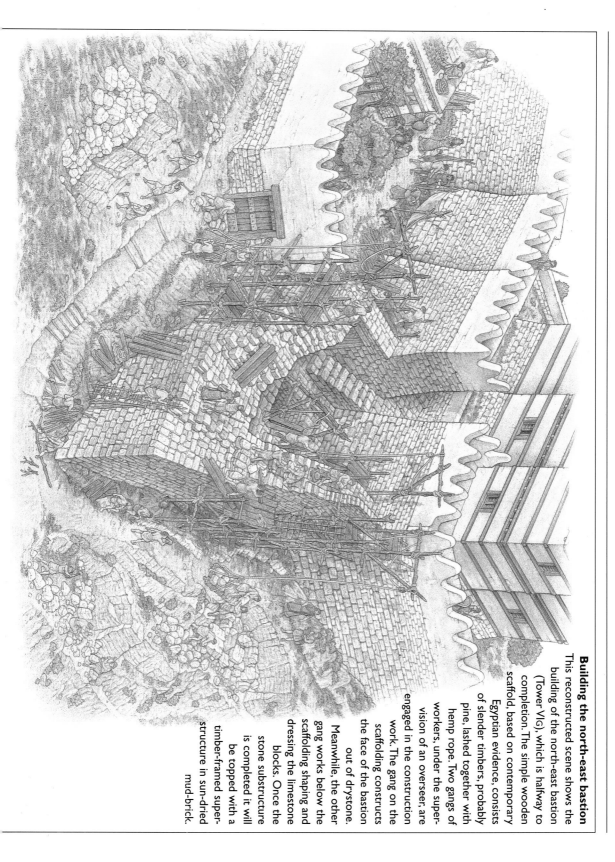

Building the north-east bastion

This reconstructed scene shows the building of the north-east bastion (Tower VIc), which is halfway to completion. The simple wooden scaffold, based on contemporary Egyptian evidence, consists of slender timbers, probably of pine, lashed together with hemp rope. Two gangs of workers, under the supervision of an overseer, are engaged in the construction work. The gang on the scaffolding constructs the face of the bastion out of drystone.

Meanwhile, the other gang works below the scaffolding shaping and dressing the limestone blocks. Once the stone substructure is completed it will be topped with a timber-framed superstructure in sun-dried mud-brick.

Dörpfeld, who discovered and excavated the fortifications of Troy VI in 1893/94, postulated that the circuit-wall was built piece by piece and gradually replaced the previous system of defence, one section at a time. With his keen eye for architectural detail, Dörpfeld was able to see that the whole undertaking required for its completion a considerable span of years during which building methods and technical skill continued to improve.

Method of construction

As was true during the Early Bronze Age at Troy, the construction of fortifications around the citadel mound appears to have been a more or less continuous activity throughout the Middle and Late Bronze Ages. That is, as was true of the pharaohs' use of pyramids during the Egyptian Old Kingdom, the rulers of Troy appear to have used the construction of fortifications surrounding their citadel as a massive, never-ending public works project.

The method of construction of the fortifications of Troy VI, especially clear in cross-section in Section 6 at the west, is entirely different from that characteristic of the Cyclopean building tradition of Mycenaean fortification architecture, that is, the use of drystone masonry of huge blocks or boulders. The roughly rectangular blocks that make up a curtain-wall, for instance, make contact not only at their exterior faces (as in Mycenaean ashlar masonry) but for the entire width of the block. Moreover, a curtain-wall as a whole is not built as two megalithic 'skins' with a fill of smaller rubble, as is typical of Cyclopean masonry, but rather consists of a solid mass of carefully fitted blocks. To increase the stability of a curtain-wall the courses were laid with a slight downward slant toward the interior.

The fortifications were bedded on foundations extending a metre or more below the contemporary ground level outside of the citadel, but the foundations rested neither on bedrock nor on virgin soil, in contrast with standard Mycenaean practice. Perhaps the leaving of a cushion of hard-packed earth between the foundations and bedrock was a conscious anti-seismic precaution, that is, as a simple shock absorber between the foundations and the rock. The latter is a more active conductor of vibrations than loose or even hard-packed earth. However, this cautionary technique does not seem to have served its purpose since the fortifications were severely damaged at the end of Troy VIh in what most authorities feel confident in identifying as a sizeable earthquake.

Curtain-walls

Little has survived of the first and second phases of wall construction, but enough is preserved to show that the curtain-walls of Troy VI were always characterised by vertical offsets. These vary between 10, 15 and 30cm in depth and recur at regular intervals of slightly over 9m, thereby breaking the circuit-wall up into distinct segments. This is a novel feature of Trojan fortification architecture, which is functional rather than decorative. The offsets show slight changes of direction in the circuit-wall thus allowing it to turn without the use of corners, the weak points in any defensive system. Another novelty of the curtain-walls is the receding slope or batter. While the internal face is vertical, the exterior face of the stone portion of a curtain-wall is strongly battered, having an inclination of approximately 1 in 3, a feature common to the fortification walls of the previous settlements but not encountered elsewhere in western Anatolia.

Completely replacing that of Early Troy VI, the circuit-wall of Middle Troy VI probably ran along the line of the south wall of the 'Pillar House' and the east wall of House VIF. In turn, the circuit-wall of Late Troy VI was built in sections to replace the preceding fortifications of Middle Troy VI. These later sections were constructed in several slightly different masonry styles and their building clearly extended over a long period of time. Thus it is possible to see the steadily increasing skill of the masons in stone cutting and joining, and the third circuit-

The north-east bastion (Tower VIɢ), the north-easternmost portion of the circuit-wall of Troy VI, looking west. This bastion, which was also accessible from the outside (Gate VIʀ), consisted of an enormous limestone substructure measuring 18 by 8m and standing at least 9m high. On top was a timber-framed superstructure of mud-brick and plaster. Built as an observation platform, the bastion dominated not only the citadel but also the whole of the lower town. To the left and abutting the bastion, are the foundations of the retaining wall of the Graeco-Roman temple precinct of Troy VIII/IX. At the right is a staircase of Troy VIII that led down to a well. (Author's collection)

wall in chronological order is by far the most ambitious and impressive. The south curtain of Section 4 is a good example of the fully developed, elegant but functional style of masonry that reveals the stonecutter's mastery of the material. The blocks are carefully fitted together at the joints, their surfaces are smooth, and neat angles are formed where the vertical offsets are cut.

The extant circuit-wall, which runs for a total distance of some 350m, is built of hard, durable limestone blocks and slabs, efficiently shaped, and solidly fitted together without the use of mortar. The faces of these blocks are rectangular almost ashlar, although the courses are not all of equal height, that is, the masonry is not isodomic. The joints between the blocks in successive courses are carefully alternated so as to maximise the strength of the construction. Large stones are freely used in the lower part, smaller material in the upper part of the wall. Once a curtain-wall had been erected, its outer, inclined face was worked over in a final dressing that gave it a relatively smooth finish from top to bottom so that it offered a very difficult surface to scale. With an average thickness of 4.75m at the base and in some places attaining 5.25m in height above the contemporary ground level outside the citadel, a timber-framed superstructure in sun-dried mud-brick originally surmounted this stone substructure. The total height of a curtain-wall therefore would have exceeded 9m.

East gateway of Troy VI

This reconstruction takes the form of an oblique aerial shot from the south, thereby showing the all-important relationship between the east tower (Tower VIH) and the east gateway (Gate VIs). Although the east tower is not actually positioned beside the east gateway, it does cover the approach, which stands some 28m away to the north. Moreover, the gateway itself takes the form of an L-shaped corridor about 2m wide and 5m long between overlapping walls. These walls overlap in such a way as to force anyone bold enough to storm the gateway to suffer exposure to missile fire from two sides at once. Also, the entrance between the walls is not located directly opposite but beyond the turn of the narrow, L-shaped corridor. This would present a further difficulty for any approaching enemy, who would be crowded into the narrow approach to the barred gate around the corner. The east gateway was clearly designed to confine and trap the enemy within a 'killing box'.

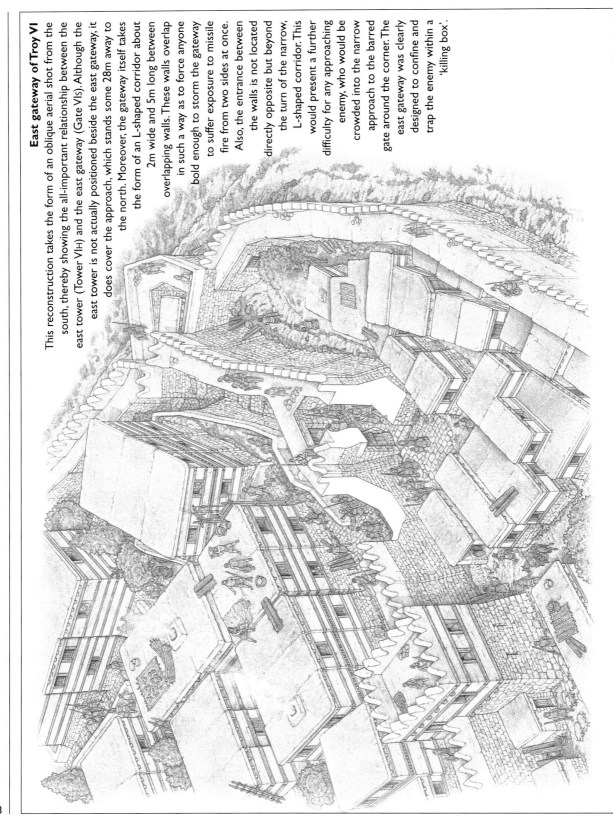

South gateway of Troy VI

This cutaway reconstruction shows the south gateway (Gate VIr) and the south tower (Tower VIi). Flanking the gateway, this massive rectangular structure replaced, probably during the final building phase (VIh), an earlier tower (Tower VIk) of smaller dimensions that stood nearly 9m to the west of the entranceway. The new tower, however, was erected directly beside the entrance, thereby giving the defenders a better vantage point from which to cover the gateway and its approach.

In the late phases of Troy VI, except in Section 1 where brick was found still *in situ*, the original mud-brick superstructure of the circuit-wall was replaced by a stone wall some 1.8 to 2m thick. This is preserved in places up to 2m in height but was originally higher, and is built consistently of neatly squared, well-fitted blocks of limestone of small size, closely resembling, both in shape and dimension, bricks of clay. Behind this strictly vertical, uppermost portion of the circuit-wall was a wall-walk 2 to 3m wide, which served as a firing platform for the defenders. It was raised some 2m above the contemporary ground level within the citadel, and was at least 2m lower than the parapet fronting it.

Towers

Although the blocks used in the curtain-walls are not Cyclopean but smaller, the fortifications of Troy VI are imposing in their total effect. This is partly due to the strong towers. These structures, which project from the external face of the circuit-wall at a number of points, clearly illustrate the architects' concern for the capability of defenders to direct enfilading fire on attackers, particularly in the vicinity of major gateways.

The east tower (Tower VIH) has a breadth of 11.25m across its front and projects more than 7m from the face of the east curtain and covers the approach to the east gateway (Gate VIs), which stands some 28m away to the north. Its north and south walls are each 2.2m thick, but the east wall is much more substantial, having a thickness of 3.4m. All three exterior faces show a slight inward batter. Inside it a chamber (8.8 by 7m) is formed and a second storey once stood over it, the floor of which was supported by heavy timber

Street leading through the lower town of Troy VI to the south gateway (Gate VIT). First revealed with the aid of magnetic prospecting, the plateau lying just south of the mound and citadel of Hisarlik was a densely inhabited area, not only in the time of Graeco-Roman Troy, but also in the Late Bronze Age. (Reproduced from Korfmann, M., et al., *Traum und Wirklichkeit: Troia*, Theiss, Stuttgart, 2001)

beams laid transversely from north to south. The floor itself probably consisted of clayey earth laid over a bed of smaller transverse timbers and rushes. Access to the room beneath was only possible at second-storey level by means of a trap door and a ladder. The upper room, however, extended westward across the top of the curtain-wall, at the inner edge of which it could be entered through a small doorway some 1.7m wide. The door was approached from outside by means of a ladder, since the threshold once stood nearly 1m above the ground level on this side. How the top was finished is difficult to judge, but it probably formed an open platform surrounded by a crenellated parapet, from which the defenders could hurl missiles at the enemy who might attack the east curtain and east gateway.

In its lower storey the east tower was constructed of large, square blocks of hard limestone, carefully fitted together in almost regular courses, and laid so that the joints did not coincide along each row. Furthermore, they were placed as an alternation of headers and stretchers. When the tower was completed its exterior face was treated with a final dressing, which produced a smoothly finished surface from top to bottom. The difference in the masonry of the tower and the east curtain point to two different building periods. A more developed method of construction is used in the tower, which is not bonded to the east curtain and therefore is evidently an added feature. Yet another difference is to be seen in the foundations. Whereas the curtain-wall was founded on a cushion of hard-packed earth, the foundations of the tower were laid directly on the bedrock, which explains the large cracks visible today. The tower was presumably built in the final building phase (VIh) as a further protection of the east gateway.

Flanking the south gateway (Gate VIт), the south tower (Tower VIı) projects 0.2m beyond the south curtain and is 9.5m wide. This massive rectangular structure replaced, probably during the final building phase (VIh), an earlier tower (Tower VIк) of smaller dimensions (7.2 by 5m) that stood nearly 9m to the west of the gateway. The new tower, however, was erected directly beside the entrance, thereby giving the defenders a better vantage point from which to cover the gateway and its approach. In its material and construction this tower is exactly like the east tower (Tower VIн).

To ensure a safe supply of water in times of stress a 10m-deep artesian well, or cistern, was sunk within the north-east bastion (Tower VIG), the north-easternmost portion of the circuit-wall also known as Section 1. The well, approximately square, has an open shaft measuring about 4.25m on a side and was lined all round with a massive stone wall some 2m thick. It extended some 2m down below the bastion floor to the bedrock, and continued down to a further depth of 7 or 8m. Too large to be a normal well, too deep for an ordinary cistern, it may have been intended to serve both purposes.

The north-east bastion, which was also accessible from the outside (Gate VIR), consists of an enormous limestone substructure measuring approximately 22 by 8m and originally stood, according to calculations made by Dörpfeld, at least 9m high above the bedrock at its northern foot. The distinctive shape of this bastion – its north corner is a sharp-edged, acute angle – makes it a very imposing structure. The well-dressed, hard, durable limestone blocks are carefully joined and placed in horizontal courses of somewhat irregular height (18 to 40cm). Here and there in some courses two thin slabs were used to make up the required height, and occasionally a polygonal style of joining appears. The outer face of the bastion was finished with a fairly smooth dressing and has the characteristic broad batter some 3m above its base. The angles of the bastion were deliberately planed and constructed with alternating headers and stretchers. On top of this massive substructure once stood a lofty timber-framed superstructure of sun-dried mud-brick. Built as an observation platform, the bastion dominated not only the citadel but also the whole of the lower town that lay below to the south and south-west.

'Well-built stronghold of Ilion'

A reconstruction panorama, looking from the south, illustrating Troy VI. One of the cutaways shows House VIM, which probably formed part of 'Priam's palace'. This two-storey building stands on the lowest terrace of the citadel mound, just within the circuit-wall of the citadel. Its inward leaning retaining-wall is 27m long and has four vertical offsets, which divide it into five distinct sections. The limestone blocks are carefully cut and closely fitted together without mortar, with larger blocks used as corner stones. The superstructure is of sun-dried mud-brick reinforced with timber and stuccoed. The flat roof is of ceiling beams covered with reeds and a thick mud plaster. Inside the L-shaped layout are several rooms. Two small rooms on the western side of the lower level are for food storage as indicated by

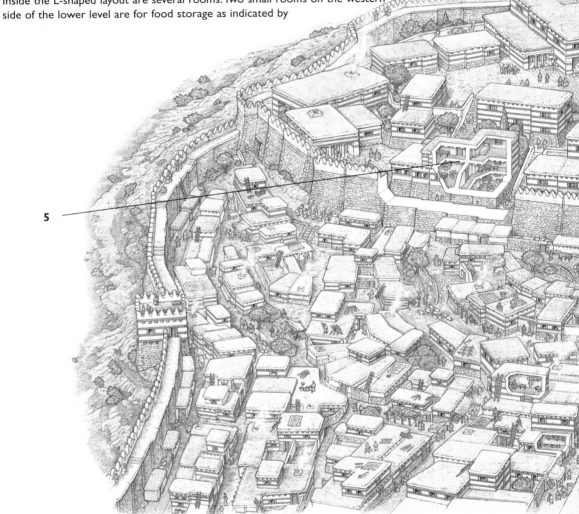

5

KEY

1. North-east bastion (Tower VIG)
2. East gateway (Gate VIS)
3. East tower (Tower VIH)
4. South tower (Tower VII)
5. House VIM
6. House VIC
7. House VIE

large storage vessels (*pithoi*). The larger room to the east is for cooking, as indicated by a preparation area in the northern corner, and eating. The upper-storey rooms are living and sleeping quarters. In contrast, the houses of the lower town are small, simple two-storied structures, standing close together and forming the continuous sides of streets. Constructed of sun-dried mud-brick reinforced with timber and plastered with mud, these stand on low, rubble-stone foundations. The inhabitants of a house generally dwell in the upper story, the lower storey having two or three rooms that serve as storerooms and workshops. The flat roof, which is timber and reed coated with thick mud plaster, is commonly used by the inhabitants to sun-dry grapes and figs, as well as serving an ideal place to relax and watch the world drift by.

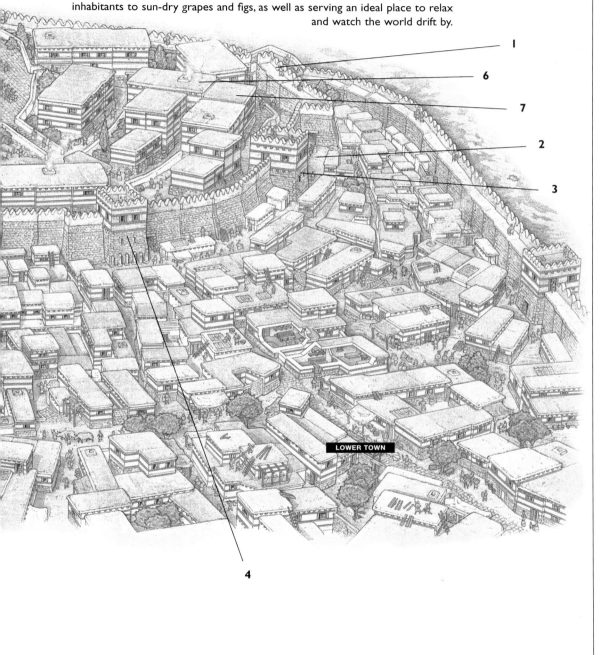

LOWER TOWN

Hattušas-Boğazköy

Hattušas-Boğazköy, from which the Hittite kings held sway over their heterogeneous empire, is surely one of the best examples of city fortification in the Late Bronze Age. The citadel was built by Hattušili I (*fl. c.* 1650 BC) on a rocky outcrop dominating the surrounding plateau. The hillside was covered by a stone glacis, a counter-response to movable siege-engines, the crest surmounted by an immense stone circuit-wall some 6.5km long and strengthened by projecting rectangular towers placed at intervals of about 30m. Beyond the circuit of the city wall were a line of crags surmounted by forts, the largest of which was the Great Fortress, a palace-cum-archive complex. Here were discovered a total of 10,000 clay tablets bearing cuneiform text, mainly in Hittite but many in Akkadian, the international language of diplomacy in the Near East. One the north, east and west the city was naturally defended by steep slopes, which were absent on the south side. Therefore, the Hittite architects designed a strong bulwark, consisting of double walls, a main curtain-wall and a lower subsidiary one thrown out some 6.5m in front of it. For surprise sorties in this weak section a corbelled passage some 71m long led under the double walls to a postern. A tower was positioned on the axis of the postern, and two flights of steps, equidistant from the tunnel opening, led up a manmade embankment to the main curtain-wall. Above the postern and built into the main curtain-wall was a gateway (Sphinx Gate).

In all there were three main gateways, each of which pierced the southern stretch of the fortification walls. Named after the larger-than-life male figure carved in relief helmeted and wielding a battle-axe, the King's Gate was a vaulted passage between two massive towers connected to both outer and inner circuit-walls. The door

continued on next page

Gateways

The circuit-wall of Late Troy VI, preserved in a great horseshoe swinging from the north-east around to the west, is pierced by five unevenly spaced gateways (Gates VIR, VIs, VIt, VIu, VIv) of different types.

A postern (Gate VIR) gave access, via a flight of four stone steps, up to the floor of the north-east bastion (Tower VIg) from the outside world. Forming the division between Sections 1 and 2, the entrance is a narrow passage 4.65m long and 1.5 to 1.7m wide. A door at the southern end of the passage would have secured the entrance, beyond which the floor of the passage ran horizontally some 2.25m and then descended the short stairway. The door, which was fitted in a wooden doorframe and turned on a pivot, could swing back into a recess in the eastern side of the passage.

As we have seen, the east tower (Tower VIh) is not actually positioned beside the east gateway (Gate VIs). Nevertheless, the gateway, separating Sections 2 and 3, takes the form of L-shaped corridor about 2m wide and 5m long between overlapping walls. These walls overlap in such a way as to force anyone bold enough to storm the gateway to suffer exposure to missile fire from two sides at once. Also, the entrance between the walls is not located directly opposite but beyond the turn of the narrow, L-shaped corridor. This presented a further difficulty for the approaching enemy, who were crowded into the narrow approach to the barred gate around the corner. By their very nature gateways are, like corners, weak points in any defensive system. The east gateway was clearly designed to confine and trap the enemy within a 'killing box'.

The principal entrance to the citadel was the south gateway (Gate VIt), which gave access from the lower town to the main thoroughfare (Street 710), which ascended to the summit of the citadel. It is notable that the main gateway to the citadel-mound has always been in the south, ever since the founding of Troy I.

The south gateway belongs to the direct-access type, in contrast to the overlapping type, as its opening is merely a gap some 3.3m wide between the vertically finished end of Section 3 and the similar beginning of Section 4. Thus forming the division between Sections 3 and 4, the architects designed this simple opening with defence as their primary concern. First, the end face of Section 4 is set back from the corresponding face of Section 3. Second, the south tower (Tower VIi), projecting some 10m from the south curtain, borders the roadway on the west. The entrance was thus flanked for a distance of more than 5m on the east and 12m on the west by solid protective works from the top of which defenders could discharge missiles in a crossfire against hostile forces attempting to storm the gateway. Although the evidence is lacking, it is assumed that a proper portal closed it.

The south-west gateway (Gate VIu) forms the division between Sections 4 and 5. Its plan is somewhat similar to that of the south gateway (Gate VIt), although its opening is slightly wider at 3.8m. It seems that the gateway was in the process of being replaced on a more ambitious scale, but for some unknown reason the project was not carried to completion. Consequently, the old gateway was no longer left open to traffic, but was sealed off by a solid and durable wall of heterogeneous stones.

A postern (Gate VIv) pierces the north-western portion of the fortifications, a simple opening between two units of the circuit-wall, Sections 5 and 6. The latter is set forward toward the west some 4.5 to 5m beyond the line of the former. The gap between the two is only some 2.5m, and the approach to the entrance from outside the citadel was evidently from the south-east via a roadway that ascended alongside Section 5 and then turned sharply eastward through the opening. Attackers attempting to storm the gateway, therefore, would have their right (unshielded) sides exposed to the missiles of the defenders on the wall above and would also have to face a frontal fire from the top of Section 6.

Outer defences

Conceivably the most important discovery of the renewed excavations at Troy under Korfmann is the exposure of an outer ring of defensive architecture consisting of a wide ditch located some 450m south-west of Section 4 of the previously known circuit-wall of Troy VI. This ditch has so far been traced for roughly 200m in a shallow east to west arc at what must have been its southernmost end. Periodically interrupted by un-excavated 'bridges' that presumably mark the locations of major entryways through this defensive circuit, the ditch is likely to have been the foundation trench for an outer circuit-wall, which has been entirely robbed out by later builders in historical times.

A short length of what is likely to be a portion of the same defensive system, but here consisting of limestone blocks still *in situ*, has been found just to the east of Section 1 at the original citadel's north-east corner. This newly discovered circuit defines what can be identified as a fortified lower town, a standard feature of Near Eastern urban centres of the third and second millennia BC. The original fortress of Troy VI thus becomes an inner royal citadel, the site of the ruler's palace complex, the settlement's chief temples, and perhaps also the residences of the ruler's principal officials and warriors.

continued from previous page

jambs were made of andesite monoliths forming the pointed arch characteristic of Hittite architecture. Still visible are the sockets for bolts and hinges and the slots for the bars that secured a massive double door. This was made of wood strengthened with bronze plates. The gateway was reached by a steep ramp that ran alongside the outer circuit-wall, positioned so as to expose the undefended right flank of attackers to the defenders on the wall. This led up to a rectangular platform some 6.5m wide. Both ramp and platform were exposed to fire from the two flanking towers. Well preserved in the southern sector, the main curtain-wall is built in Cyclopean masonry with huge, roughly worked limestone blocks dressed so as to fit together without mortar. This wall consists of an inner and outer shell with cross-walls between, forming a series of rectangular spaces filled with rubble – a characteristic of Hittite fortification walls wherever they are found. The upper parts of the wall have not survived, but can be reconstructed with the aid of Egyptian art. The height of the stone wall that formed the substructure was about 6m and this was overlaid with a superstructure of sun-dried mud-brick. The defensive strength of this system of fortifications is obvious and the Hittites were undoubtedly masters of military engineering.

Close-up shot of the east tower (Tower VIh) of Troy VI showing one of the large vertical earthquake cracks on the wall facing the east gateway (Gate VIs). The final building phase (VIh) was severely damaged by an earthquake, as is evident from the large vertical cracks in the surviving fortification walls. Nevertheless, Dörpfeld found evidence for fire or fires at various places in the destruction level of Troy VIh and saw this destruction as the work of men. (Author's collection)

'Woman of To-ro-ja'

There is a significant and growing body of evidence to show that the Mycenaeans of the 14th and 13th centuries BC, the heyday of their civilisation, were involved in armed forays on the shores of western Anatolia. Indeed it is fair to say that we now have a plausible context for the tale told by Homer. In the Linear B tablets from Pylos particular groups of women are recorded doing menial tasks such as grinding grain, carding flax and spinning wool. Their ration quotas suggest that they were numbered in the hundreds. Many are distinguished by ethnic adjectives, presumably denoting the places they came from, and though some of these are still not understood, several of the women come from eastern Aegean islands or the western seaboard of Anatolia – Knidos, Miletos, Lemnos, Halikarnassos, Chios and AS-WI-JA. The last name frequently occurs at Pylos, Knossos and Mycenae (e.g. PY Ab 315, KN Sc 261, MY Au 657), and seems to denote an area originally known as Asia, that is Lydia (*Assuwa* in Hittite). Recorded on one tablet from Pylos (PY Ep 705.6) there is even the enigmatic name TO-RO-JA ('woman of Troy').

The Pylos tablets name 700 women, with their 400 girls and 300 boys who 'belong to them'. Some of the ethnic groups are sizeable: '21 women of Knidos (KI-NI-DI-JA), with their 12 girls and ten boys' (PY Ab 189) or '16 women of Miletos (MI-RA-TI-JA), with their three girls and seven boys' (PY Ab 573). These

descriptions often use the term LA-WI-AI-AI, 'captives', which is the same word used by Homer (*Iliad* 20.193) to describe women (*leiadas de gynaikas*) seized by Achilles at Lyrnessos during a predatory foray south of Troy. It is a remarkable fact that Homer also names a number of islands in the eastern Aegean as homes of women taken on Achaian raids, including Lesbos, Skyros and Tenedos (*Iliad* 9.128–30, 270–72, 664–65, 11.625–27).

Of sheep and women

A few of the women listed on the Pylos tablets are domestics, such as 'bath-pourers', but the majority seem to have been workers who were producing woollen and linen cloth of various kinds. Indeed, textiles for trading purposes appear to have been a main source of Mycenaean wealth. At Knossos alone, where a third of all the tablets in the archive are concerned with sheep and wool, records for a single season list at least 70,000 to 80,000 sheep (KN Od series). The vast majority of these are wethers (neutered males), which give the finest fleeces, but no milk and only tough meat. At upward of a pound and a half of wool per sheep, by the Mycenaeans' own reckoning, we come up with some 60 tons of wool – a count that checks well against the Knossos accounts of cloth made. This was no cottage industry.

These Linear B tablets provide vivid evidence for the predatory nature of Mycenaean activity in the eastern Aegean. The women were either captured during seaborne raids, or brought from slave traders in entrepôts such as Miletos. The fact that they are usually mentioned with their children but not with men implies the familiar

raiding pattern of predatory warbands, where the men are killed and the women carried off. A clay tablet from Pylos (PY Ab 555) speaks of rations sent to textile workers and their children. The inscribed text, which reads from left to right, says:

This ivory plaque from the sanctuary of Artemis Orthia in Sparta, dated to the second half of the 7th century BC, depicts a warship in low relief with her prow to the right ready to depart (National Archaeological Museum, Athens, Inv. No. 15362). As the ship is being made ready to make sail, five hoplites have already taken their places next to the gunwale, while two deckhands unfurl the sail. Another is fishing from the prow, while yet another is squatting on the ram of the ship relieving himself. A female figure standing on the gangplank in a trailing garment grasps the hand of a naked man standing in the stern, touching his shoulder with her left hand. The Spartans were notorious landlubbers, so the scene could illustrate a celebrated myth such as the abduction of Helen, a woman of peerless grace, charm and beauty (the face that launched a thousand ships) by Paris. (Author's collection).

PU-RO RA-PI-TI-RYA: WOMEN 38, KO-WA 20, KO-WO 19.
WHEAT 16, FIGS 16
Pylos loom-workers: 38 women, 20 girls, 19 boys.
Wheat: 16 measures. Figs: 16 measures

In Homeric Greek the terms for 'girls' and 'boys' are *kourai* and *kouroi* respectively. The Linear B symbol for WOMAN is an ideogram showing her head and long skirt. The numerals operate on the decimal system, though the weights and measures show traces of the Babylonian system of division in 60 parts.

The *Iliad* and the Linear B texts complement each other here in a remarkable way, and it is safe to assume that Homer is here preserving a genuine Late Bronze Age memory. Right from the opening of the *Iliad* (1.366–69, 29–31) Agamemnon makes the following boasts:

We went against Thebes, the sacred city of Eëtion,
and the city was sacked, and carried everything back to this place,
and the sons of the Achaians made a fair distribution,
and for Atreus' son they chose out Chryseis of the fair cheeks …
The girl [Chryseis] I will not give back; sooner will old age come upon her
in my own house, in Argos, far from her own land, going
up and down by the loom and being in my bed as my companion.

Being carried off appears to be a constant hazard for women during Mycenaean times; especially those living near the sea. A Phoenician serving-women in the *Odyssey* (15.426–29) reports her entry into bondage thus:

[M]en from Taphos [a Greek island],
pirates, caught me and carried me away as I came back
home from the fields, and carried me to this place and sold me
here in this man's house, being paid a fair price for me.

Many Achaian princes kept captured women as servants and bed-partners. In the former occupation they spent much of their time spinning the wool produced by their masters' flocks and weaving garments, bedding, seat-covers and wraps.

Sackers of cities

The Mycenaeans were warlike and brutal, and it did not need many ships full of armed raiders to threaten and sack a small coastal settlement and enslave its women. A generation before the Achaians sailed against Troy under the leadership of Agamemnon, Herakles, leading the crews of six vessels, stormed Laomedon's Troy and 'widowed the streets' (*Iliad* 5.638–42, cf. 14.250–1). Other versions say that Herakles came with 18 ships (Diodoros 4.32.2, Apollodoros 2.6.4), but all agree that he brought only a small force to destroy Troy.

Small groups of predators, chieftains and their personal warbands, appear at many places in the 13th-century BC Near Eastern texts. The large city of Ugarit (Ras Shamra), which had been an important trade centre in western Syria since

The Silver Siege Rhyton (LH IA) from Shaft Grave IV of Grave Circle A at Mycenae depicts, in repoussé relief, the siege of a fortified coastal town (National Archaeological Museum, Athens, Inv. No. 481). The raiders land from the sea, as indicated by the stylised wave pattern, and proceed to attack the mud-brick fortifications, which surmount a rocky eminence. The naked defenders of the town, armed only with slings and bows, seem to belong to some 'barbaric' tribe, while the attackers are clearly Mycenaeans as shown by their helmets and shields. That they came by ship is indicated by one valuable clue, for a man, clad in plumed helmet and short-sleeved tunic, holds a tiller and, evidently, is a helmsman. Amongst the defenders are female onlookers who are anxiously watching the course of the battle on the seashore from the walls of the town. An intriguing parallel can be found in one of the most famous excursus in the *Iliad* (18.478–607), namely the Shield of Achilles. On Achilles' new shield the city at war faces a sack and the loss of its property, and while it waits, its men prepared themselves for an armed sortie while 'their beloved wives and their little children stood on the rampart' (*Iliad* 18.509–14). (Author's collection)

the Middle Bronze Age, was destroyed by fire at the end of the Late Bronze Age and was not, unlike Troy VI, reoccupied. As well as numerous arrowheads, the destruction level contained some 100 clay tablets and so from this site we have documents written prior to Ugarit's demise. One of these tablets (RS 20.238) is a letter from Hammurabi, the last king of Ugarit, to the king of *Alasiya* (Cyprus):

> Behold the enemy's ships are already here, and they have set fire to my towns, and have done very great damage in the country. Does not my father know all my troops and chariots (?) are in the Hittite country, and that all my ships are in the land of Lycia and have not yet returned? So that the country is abandoned to itself … Consider this my father, there are seven ships of the enemy that have come and done very great damage upon us.

Thus with just seven ships the anonymous raiders sail in, wreak havoc and raze settlements and then sail away. Not long afterwards (*c.* 1185 BC) Ugarit itself was sacked and burned.

In the Hittite texts from Hattušas-Boğazköy there appears the term 'Land of Ahhiyawa', a powerful seafaring state ruled by a 'Great King'. In one important document, the so-called Tawagalawas Letter (KUB 14.3) written by Hattušili III (*fl.* 1250 BC) to the unnamed king of *Ahhiyawa*, the main subject is the buccaneering adventures of a certain Piyamaradu. Piyamaradu, a powerful renegade, is raiding Hittite lands apparently in collusion with Tawagalawas, a brother of the king of *Ahhiyawa*. *Millawanda* is the point of departure for these seaborne raids, and eventually Hattušili enters the city, from which Tawagalawas and Piyamaradu

These regimented figures depicted on Side A of the Warrior Vase (LH IIIb/c), found by Schliemann at Mycenae, are the best representations of warriors from the Trojan War period (National Archaeological Museum, Athens, Inv. No. 1426). Used for mixing water and wine, this late Mycenaean *krater* is decorated with a singular frieze of bearded warriors wearing plumed and horned helmets, body-armour and greaves, and carry shields that are round except for a scallop on the bottom and are armed with short spears. Note a small bag hangs from the spear, which probably carried the soldier's campaign rations and personal effects. (Author's collection)

have fled overseas to *Ahhiyawa*. Though demanding the extradition of Piyamaradus, Hattušili is anxious not to provoke an international incident and assures the addressee that he will despatch a royal kinsman as a hostage to guarantee safe conduct of Piyamaradu from *Ahhiyawa* to the Hittite kingdom and back. Formerly a high-ranking subject of Hattušili, Piyamaradu had evidently turned freebooter as a protégé of the king of *Ahhiyawa*. It was in this capacity that he was now making piratical raids upon the Hittite king's vassal states of western Anatolia.

Hittitologists are generally convinced that the place-name 'Land of *Ahhiyawa*' refers to the Mycenaean world, or at least to part of that world. It is no mere coincidence, therefore, the similarity between the name *Ahhiyawa* and the Homeric designation of the Late Bronze Age Greeks as *Achaiwoí*. Thus *Millawanda*, which is most probably Miletos (MI-RA-TI-JA in the Linear B texts) where the presence of Mycenaean colonists is indicated by Mycenaean-type burials and domestic architecture, serves as their main base in western Anatolia. And it is this settlement that provides the means for continuing Mycenaean or Mycenaean-sponsored encroachment on Hittite subject territory.

Intriguingly, the archaeological evidence for the destruction of Thermi on Lesbos, the island's main city and one of the largest Bronze Age settlements in the Aegean, can be compared with the Hittite account, the so-called Manapa-Tarhunda Letter (KUB 19.5), of the attack on Lesbos (*Lazpas* in Hittite) by Piyamaradu. A thriving trading port on the eastern side of the island and thus close to the shores of the Troad, Thermi shared the culture of Troy VI and was sacked and burned by hostile invaders at the same time, that is, around 1250 BC. It would be no surprise to learn that we could also associate the destruction of Thermi with the Homeric tale of Achilles' sack of 'strong–founded Lesbos' (*Iliad* 9.129, 271).

The title Mycenaean sea-raiders most coveted, if we can trust Homer, was 'sacker of cities'. In the Homeric epics it was the warlord's greatest claim to glory. Achilles, Odysseus, Nestor ('in my youth I was one') and even Pallas Athena, the pro-Achaian goddess of conventional warfare, bear the title of 'sacker of cities' (*Iliad* 2.278, 5.765, 21.550, *Odyssey* 13.359, 14.447 etc.). In the *Iliad* the sacker of cities does not destroy and slaughter to increase his political power, on the contrary, he sacks cities to gain booty, treasure, horses, cattle, gold, silver, fine armour and weapons and, last but not least, women (*Iliad* 9.278–81, 591–94, 16.830–32). The possibility of men being enslaved and women killed never arises. We should bear in mind that it was the seizure of one woman, Helen of Sparta, which was the *casus belli* of the Trojan War. Already at the very beginning of the *Iliad* there is a pernicious quarrel between Achilles and Agamemnon over a woman who is part of the spoil. Time and time again Homer tells of the fight for 'the city and its women' (*Iliad* 6.95, 18.265, *Odyssey* 11.403, 24.113 etc.). When Achilles tells Odysseus of the 23 cities he has sacked he mentions only booty and women as his gain (*Iliad* 9.325–31, cf. 18.28–29). Men and real estate are destroyed; women and movable property are taken as spoils. Winning profit and prestige, this is what makes him proud and gives him fame.

OPPOSITE The seer Laocoön rightly warned the Trojans against the Wooden Horse (as Kassandra also does), telling them not to bring the artful gift into their city. His story is dramatically told by Virgil (*Aeneid* 2.40-56, 199-233), who has Laocoön give the (much-quoted) warning, 'I fear the Greeks, especially when they bear gifts' (*Aeneid* 2.49). He then cast his spear into the Horse's flank. The image boomed and echoed, sounding suspiciously hollow, but at that moment the Greek Sinon, pretending to be a deserter, came on the scene and persuaded the Trojans that the Horse was a genuine offering to Athena. Their belief in Sinon's words was strengthened when they saw what happened next to Laocoön and his two sons; they were strangled by sea snakes sent by the gods who favoured the Greeks. In art, Laocoön is best known for this marble statuary group in the Vatican (Cortile di Belvedere 74), which depicts him and his two sons in their death throes, crushed by the snakes. It was in the palace of Titus in the time of Pliny the Elder, who declared (*Natural History* 36.37) that it surpassed all other works of painting and sculpture. This masterpiece of antiquity, a Roman copy of a Rhodian bronze of the late 2nd century BC, was one of the major discoveries of the Italian Renaissance. Unearthed from the ruins of Titus' palace in 1506, it was to be much admired and serve as a source of inspiration for a number of notable artists – it would be copied, for instance, by Titian, El Greco, Bernini, Caravaggio and Rubens. (Author's collection)

The Wooden Horse of Troy

We leave the *Iliad* at Hector's tomb and open the *Odyssey* to find Troy sacked and the Achaians still on their wandering homeward way. Homer mentions the Wooden Horse in three brief, exciting, but almost casual passages (*Odyssey* 4.265–74, 8.487–520, 11.523–32), while Aeschylus (*Agamemnon* 823–28) and Euripides (*Trojan Women* 511–30, *Hecuba* 905–31) show us some supreme moments. But it is the Roman poet Virgil (70–19 BC) who takes us to the heart of the matter. He uses the traditional setting for the sack of Troy, a moonlit night, with the Trojans all asleep as the Horse ejected its dangerous brood. Virgil might have been at Troy itself: here is no academic fighting, but the real thing – the flames, the chaos, the forlorn hope, the bravery of the old, the endless line of captive women.

Harbinger of doom

In one scene in the second book of Virgil's *Aeneid* we are deeply conscious of the Horse's presence throughout. First the Horse appears; then the Trojan seer, Laocoön, gives his warning; the Greek 'fugitive', Sinon, tells his tale; Laocoön and his two sons perish; the Horse is taken into Troy, and its menace is fulfilled. For Virgil the Horse is completely sinister, without pedigree, appearing from nowhere. Late Greek epic shows the Horse in glorious Technicolor.

Already in Euripides it is the 'gold-decked thing' (*Trojan Women* 520). Tryphiodoros (*Taking of Ilios* 57–89), on the other hand, gives it a mane of purple and gold, blood-red amethyst eyes set with green beryl, rows of white jagged teeth, and hooves of bronze. While Quintus Smyrnaeus (*Fall of Troy* 12.149–50) sees it as swift and mettlesome, so alive that it seems to neigh. But Virgil keeps free from temptation. For him the Horse is a practical and deadly instrument of war, the doom of Troy.

According to the anonymous author of the *Ilias Parva* (Apollodoros *Epitome* 5.14) the Horse held 3,000 men, a figure even medieval tradition reduced to a thousand. Homer says 'all the best of the Argives' (*Odyssey* 8.512) were in it but names five only. Stesichoros (*fr.* 199) gave 100, Apollodoros (*Epitome* 5.14) 50. Quintus Smyrnaeus names 30, 'with many others' (*Fall of Troy* 12.314–30), and Tryphiodoros (*Taking of Ilios* 152–83) lists 23 men. But Virgil's mountain-huge animal held nine men only (*Aeneid* 2.261–64).

So a single Horse captured Troy, as Philostratos (*Life of Apollonios of Tyana* 5.26) says, and Dio Chrysostom (*Orations* 64.22) equates it with the Great King of Persia Cyrus the Great as a conqueror of cities. The Horse can, of course, be explained away as a ship. Apollodoros (*Epitome* 5.15) describes the process of putting men inside the Horse with the word *embibázo*, a term regularly used of putting men on board a ship. Homer does say ships 'serve as horses' (*Odyssey* 4.708) for men crossing the sea. Euripides compares the Horse to a 'dark ship' (*Trojan Women* 539), and in an inspired

moment Tryphiodoros calls it a 'vessel' (*Taking of Ilios* 185), while Quintus Smyrnaeus (*Fall of Troy* 12.427–34) elaborately likens its entry into Troy to a ship launching. Or again, the Horse was really a siege machine, a view held by two early critics, Pliny the Elder (*Natural History* 7.202) and Servius (2.15). Pausanias even goes as far as to say that 'anyone who does not think the Trojans were utterly stupid will have realised that the Horse was really an engineer's device for breaking down the walls' (1.23). Servius offers other suggestions, such as the gate opened by the traitor Antenor had a painted horse upon it, or the Horse was in fact a mountain called Hippios, behind which the Greeks lurked prior to the assault. In more recent times it has been held to be a theriomorphic manifestation of Poseidon the Earth-shaker and a siege-engine of Assyrian type.

The 'Assyrian Horse'

Geniuses of siege warfare, the Assyrians commonly employed a device known as a 'wall-fly' whenever they laid siege to a city or fortified town. The palace bas-reliefs depicting siege-engines clearly illustrate them equipped with a drill or pair of drills some 5m in length and topped with a spear-shaped head. The device itself was mounted on a light wooden framework some 5 to 8m long and 1.5 to 2m wide and covered by various materials, inside which the crew of the machine worked. The whole structure was mounted on wheels, usually four in number, which enabled it to be advanced up to the enemy's walls along a ramp constructed of several layers of stone or logs tightly packed with earth. During the reign of Tiglath-Pileser III (745–727 BC) and in the Sargonid period (726–705 BC) the machine was more or less cubic in shape and was provided with a tower in front and, as a rule, the whole device was mounted on four wheels. Here it is important to bear in mind that the Wooden Horse was mobile, being equipped with wheels attached to its hooves (Tryphiodoros *Taking of Ilios* 100, Quintus Smyrnaeus *Fall of Troy* 12.424–27, cf. Virgil *Aeneid* 2.35–36).

The framework of an Assyrian siege-engine was covered with a protective material, probably canvas, felt or hide (Nimrud, Central Palace [British Museum 118901, 118903]). Of particular interest are recommendations of the 4th-century BC Greek soldier-scholar Aineias Taktikos (33.3) for protecting flammable wooden towers and parapets from fire by covering them with felt or hide and this was undoubtedly the case with these Assyrian siege-engines. Aineias (34.1) also suggests the use of vinegar to douse out fires, the vinegar also having the added property of making it much harder for fires to restart. The 'wall-flies' depicted in British Museum 118901, for instance, are each shown with a crewmember who is armed with a ladle from which he is pouring water or, perhaps, vinegar. The possibility that these coverings were made of soft material is clearly evident in the Lachish Relief, a remarkable series of bas-reliefs commemorating the siege and

Fixed or mobile Assyrian siege-engines, equipped with a massive iron-shod drill, first appear in bas-reliefs during the reign of Ashurnasirpal II (883–859 BC). These machines were probably constructed *in situ* since they utilised large numbers of infantry shields and, on occasions, chariot wheels as well. By the reign of Tiglath-Pileser III (745–727 BC), the siege-engine had developed into a lighter and more mobile weapon. The body of the machine appears to be made of three sections, front, middle and rear, most probably of wicker covered in ox-hide. The front was usually taller than the rest, forming a turret with a window. The whole structure was moved on four or six wheels. The drill (or pair of drills) was long and thin, protruding from high up the front of the machine and ending in a large spearhead. This was inserted between the courses of the wall's brickwork and moved from side to side, pulling out the mud-bricks and thus weakening the wall, as we witness in this bas-relief from the North-West Palace of Ashurnasirpal II at Nimrud. The size of the crew is not readily apparent from the bas-reliefs, but one archer and a man with a ladle are shown in a number of examples and, perhaps, a further three or four men would have been required to operate the drill itself. (Author's collection)

conquest of the Judaean city of Lachish by Sennacherib (r. 704–681 BC). Here each siege-engine is protected by a covering of hides fastened by a series of loops and pegs, and equipped with one long spear-shaped drill (Nineveh, Palace of Sennacherib Room XXXVI [British Museum 124906, 124907]). Moreover, they were somewhat animal-like in shape with a body and neck, and contained men inside.

Although siege-engines were not shown on the Assyrian representations prior to the reign of Ashurnasirpal II (883–859 BC), documentary evidence from Mari (Tal Al-Hariri, Syria) and Hattušas-Boğazköy does indicate that such machines were already in use as early as the 18th century BC. These documents also tell us these machines were named after animals: the 'wild ass' at Mari and the 'wooden one-horned animal' at Hattušas-Boğazköy (Dossin 1950: Letter 131, Jean 1950: Letter 7). A similar device is depicted in the tomb of the Egyptian XII Dynasty noble Khety at Beni-Hasan (Tomb 17). It has a single long-shafted weapon with, presumably, a hefty metal point, which required three men to wield. This is shown operating directly beneath the mud-brick ramparts of a well-fortified town, the crew being protected by a sort of movable hut. A similar mud-brick superstructure surmounted the fortifications of Troy VI, and, as the evidence suggests, siege-engines were often named after animals and invariably looked like them. The Wooden Horse, therefore, can be rationalised as a siege device in a mobile, horse-shaped housing in which men could operate.

The siege of Lachish

The Old Testament simply says that 'King Sennacherib of Assyria laid siege to Lachish' (*II Chronicles* 32:9, cf. *II Kings* 18:14, 17, 19:8, *Isaiah* 36:2, 37:8). More informative, however, are the extant Assyrian texts that cover Sennacherib's Palestinian campaign of 701 BC, a punitive expedition that was directed against a confederation of rebel kingdoms headed by Hezekiah of Judah. Here we read (Prism of Sennacherib, ii.27–iii.49, cf. *II Kings* 18:13) that the Assyrian king:

laid siege to 46 of his [Hezekiah's] strong cities, walled forts and to the countless small villages in their vicinity and conquered [them] by means of well-stamped [earth-] ramps, and great

wall-flies brought near [to the walls combined with] the attack by foot soldiers [using] mines, breeches as well as sapper work.

The archaeological level representing the city of Lachish (Level III) besieged by Sennacherib has been securely identified along with the main siege ramp complete with evidence of the fierce battle and ensuing destruction of the site. Situated against the south-west corner of the outer circuit-wall, the ramp is composed of enormous amounts of rubble heaped on the surface of the open area at the foot of the tell and laid against its slope. The upper layer of the ramp consists of stones bound with hard mortar. This layer was the mantle of

the ramp, added on top of the loose boulders in order to create a compact surface. The whole structure – according to existing surface remains – was relatively wide and probably fan-shaped, narrowing to its apex at the base of the outer circuit-wall, a wall of sun-dried mud-brick resting on stone foundations some 3.5 to 4m thick. It is estimated that the overall width of the ramp at its bottom was about 55 to 60m and its height about 16m. The Lachish Relief depicts each 'wall-fly' standing on a track made of wooden logs, and it is assumed, therefore, that a narrow track of logs or wooden beams was laid along the sloping surface of the ramp for each attacking siege-machine to enable its smooth ascent to the top.

The 'Wooden Horse'

This reconstruction takes the form of a close-up shot of the 'Wooden Horse' operating directly beneath the battlements of Troy. The Trojan defenders are armed with missile weapons, namely slings and composite bows, and firebrands, while a number of the Mycenaeans are busy operating the siege machine itself. The Mycenaean assault-party carries scaling-ladders and is rushing forward, while archers, likewise armed with composite bows, and slingers provide supporting fire from behind makeshift wickerwork pavises.

Aineias' drill

The three-man crew of the Egyptian siege-machine described above are poking at rather than battering against the ramparts. In his treatise *How to Survive under Siege*, the Arcadian soldier-of-fortune Aineias Taktikos (*fl.* 350 BC) offers us a glimpse of a similar device in operation (32.5–6). The implication here is that the hand-held drill or borer (*tripanon*), as opposed to the battering ram (*krios*), was a far better device for breaching walls of mud-brick. In their edition of the treatise Hunter and Handford (1927: 221, cf. Whitehead 1990: 194–95) supposed Aineias was using the term *tripanon* for the nose of the battering ram. However, this left them unable to explain the manoeuvre with the counter-ram (*anti-krios*), which is evidently used to combat the drill by breaking through the wall from the inside and snap off the point of the enemy drill, the former, according to Aineias, being 'the stronger of the two' (32.7). If we assume that Aineias is speaking throughout of mud-brick walls and the drill proper, the problem is less formidable, for the opening of a small aperture in a mud-brick wall cannot have been very serious, and the hole could quickly be filled. In fact the Plataians, according to Thucydides (2.75.6), used this very means to thwart the earth-mound that had been thrown up against their city wall by the Peloponnesians during the siege of 429 BC.

Although he obviously knows what he is talking about with regard to siege tactics, Aineias Taktikos can be frustratingly vague when it comes to technical detail. He thus says nothing of the drill's actual construction. The Roman military engineer M. Vitruvius Pollio (*fl.* 50 BC), on the other hand, is much more lucid on this subject. For he describes a drill that consists of an iron-pointed beam, some 25m long, which moves back and forth on rollers along a wooden trough, thereby rendering 'its movement quicker and more violent' (10.13.7). This particular device is housed within an arched framework covered in rawhide and, thus, is not too dissimilar to that employed by the Egyptians and, presumably, explains by example the siege-machine used by the Mycenaeans at Troy.

Alternative means

Bronze Age siege tactics, however, also included stratagems of deceit. The Wooden Horse, therefore, could be explained as a simple deception motif, which is worth discussing if only to be rejected.

According to an Egyptian tale, that known as *The Taking of Joppa* (Papyrus Harris 500 [British Museum 10060]), when the forces of Thutmose III (r. 1479–1425 BC) failed to capture Joppa (Jaffa) by traditional siege methods, the city was ultimately taken by a stratagem reminiscent of Ali Baba. Djehuti, the pharaoh's general, conceals 200 of his soldiers in 200 wicker baskets, fills 300 other baskets with cords and fetters and loads 500 other soldiers with these baskets, and sends them into the city in the character of captives. Once inside the gates and night had fallen, the bearers liberate and arm their comrades, take the place without a fight, and make all the inhabitants prisoners.

Whatever the truth of this story, and there are many scholars who feel that it is pure fable rather than actual fact, Djehuti himself was a historical character who

A large terracotta *pithos*, from an early 7th-century BC tomb on Mykonos, Cyclades, decorated with a relief depicting the siege of Troy (Archaeological Museum, Mykonos, Inv. No. 2240). This is one of the earliest surviving examples depicting the Wooden Horse, which appears, complete with wheels, on the neck of the *pithos*. Seven of the Achaian warriors have already begun to climb out of the hollow body of the Horse, while seven others, peering from window-like openings, wait their turn. Below the Horse three horizontal rows of panels spanning the vessel's upper body continues the narrative. Having already slain the Trojan men, the Greeks, like the Achaians of epic poetry, are now enslaving their mothers, wives and daughters. (Archaeological Museum, Mykonons, photograph P. Hatzidakis)

The Trojan Horse as illustrated in the late 15th-century manuscript of Raoul Lefèvre's French version of the medieval story of the Sack of Troy. The hatch of the Horse is open and a ladder is ready for the descent of the Greeks inside. While the Horse is shown standing at a breach in the walls beside a gateway named *La Porte Dardane* or the Dardanian Gate, in the background the Greeks, who wear medieval plate armour, have already started butchering the inhabitants in *La Ville de Troia*, or the City of Troy. (Reproduced from Sevinç, N., *Troia*, A Turizm Press, Istanbul, 1996)

The modern replica of the Wooden Horse of Troy situated at the entrance of the site of Troy. Constructed in 1974, this tourist attraction has become an icon of Troy ever since. When it was built reference was made to the various depictions on ancient pottery and descriptions of the ancient writers. (Author's collection)

served Thutmose III. In fact, the general's tomb at Thebes contains an inscription, the so-called Northampton Stela, describing his role in the pharaoh's Meggido campaign (*c.* 1457 BC). Thus there is little reason to doubt the fact that Djehuti was sent by Thutmose to capture Joppa, although, admittedly, he took the stronghold by an extraordinary ruse that would perhaps later be the origin of a number of tales. Still, Aineias Taktikos (29.3–10) cites the trick of smuggling weapons into a city so as to facilitate its capture by enemy forces during a public festival. Concealed in containers and cargoes and moved into the city, the arms and armour were then issued to fifth columnists during the night of the festivities, the opportune moment to seize control as the unsuspecting citizens 'had become thoroughly drunk' (29.8).

The Trojans celebrated what they thought was their final victory and dragged the Wooden Horse into Troy. That night, after most of Troy was asleep or in a drunken stupor, Sinon unsealed the belly of the Horse and let the Greek warriors out, who then opened the gates to the waiting Greek Army. And so Troy succumbed to fire and sword.

'The castle of Priam blazing'

Troy VI was the *loci* of a maritime power on a promontory in a marine embayment adjacent to the strategic straits of the Dardanelles (cf. Homer's 'guardian of the Hellespont'). Exercising control over the straits, the Trojans probably proved troublesome to many seafarers and thereby protected themselves against possible retaliation as the remarkable fortification system indicates. Reefs along the European side of the narrow strait as well as strong currents and stubborn winds would have proved of benefit to the controller. At a time when Mycenaean contacts were spreading throughout the eastern Mediterranean, there can be no doubt the warlike Mycenaeans were all too familiar with the wealthy, fortified settlement near the straits; the substantial amount of their ceramics found here attest it.

Against the wind

Funnelled through the straits in a south-westerly direction, a current runs through the Dardanelles at an average speed of 2.5 to 3 knots (cf. Homer's 'swift-flowing Hellespont'). In order to reach the Sea of Marmara, therefore, a constant rowing speed of at least 5 knots was necessary to successfully pass up the Dardanelles. A further complication to the outward-flowing current is the strong and nearly ceaseless winds, which usually blow from the north-east in a south-westerly direction parallel to the current. The daily average speed of these winds is a little over 16km/h (cf. Homer's 'windy Ilion'). Such north-east winds, which the modern Greeks call the *meltémi*, remain prevalent from spring to early autumn, the months best suited to navigation in the Aegean. For the ancient mariner, with his rig of a single sail hung square on a horizontal yard, the technique of sailing close-hauled to the wind or beating up against it was unfeasible.

The site of a possible Mycenaean cemetery, Beşik Tepe lies within a few metres of Beşika Bay, a shallow embayment with a gently sloping sandy beach. Entrance to the bay is open and not blocked by reefs. The bay itself is sheltered from the prevailing north-easterly winds and remains just in the lee of the Dardanelles current. It even has freshwater sources. Moreover, evidence from recent palaeogeographical studies reveal that in the Bronze Age the sea reached far inland beyond the present shoreline and, like the bay in front of Troy, Beşika Bay has silted and filled in the course of time. Located only 8km south-west of Troy, this bay once provided the first natural harbour south of the entrance to the Dardanelles. Often identified in the past as the most likely anchorage of any seaborne force attacking Troy, the bay also served as the logical stopping point for ships seeking to pass up the Dardanelles but forced to wait for the necessary favourable winds. The *Black Sea Pilot* (1908: 7) speaks of the summer wind from the Dardanelles sometimes continuing for so long that it is not uncommon to see 200 or 300 vessels in the 11km-wide channel between Tenedos and the mainland or in the other havens, waiting for a change of wind.

Compelled to bide their time awaiting weather conditions favourable for the journey up the Dardanelles, it is not hard to imagine Bronze Age seafarers beaching their ships along the sandy shore of Beşika Bay. But these were Trojan waters. Here the Trojans could exact levies from, and provide goods and services to, the hapless crews of stranded vessels. Well-built Troy may have grown wealthy from tribute and trade – and long been a thorn in the side of merchant entrepreneurs like the predatory Mycenaeans. To draw a line between maritime trade and piracy is difficult in any period, and the building of the increasingly

The Trojans assault the Mycenaean encampment at Besika Bay
Having beached their ships at Besika Bay, the Mycenaean war party hastens to construct a rampart around their encampment. This reconstruction depicts a determined Trojan assault upon the Mycenaean defences prior to their completion, with the Trojan warriors intent on firing the Mycenaean ships. The Mycenaeans are obviously caught off guard, so we witness a chaotic scene with some warriors dropping their work tools and rushing for their arms and armour, as others emerge from their shelters with bleary eyes.

stronger fortifications during the heyday of Troy VI may have been in response to an excessive interest in the prosperous coastal settlement on the part of Mycenaean seafarers. But when attack came, neither economic prosperity nor strong walls were to be of any use as shown by the fate of Troy VI when it fell to raiders and was brutally sacked.

The stuff of legend

The impressive fortification walls of Troy VI, as excavated, mostly belong to the late phases of the settlement. Troy VIh was a settlement at the height of its wealth and glory and architectural development. Troy VIIa, on the other hand, was rather nondescript. The pre-Blegen view, put forward by Dörpfeld (1902: 181–82), was that Troy VIh, albeit damaged by an earthquake, had been sacked. Dörpfeld had found evidence for a great conflagration at various places in the destruction level of Troy VIh and had interpreted the destruction as the work of men, not of nature. But while Blegen (1953: 330–32) acknowledged that Troy VIh had been burned, he argued that this proud settlement was the victim of a catastrophic earthquake and not warlike action. For him the attackers had sacked the humdrum Troy VIIa.

Blegen's arguments were given close scrutiny by Michael Wood (1985: 225–30) and, following up some of Wood's ideas, Donald Easton (1985: 188–95) reviewed in detail the evidence upon which Blegen based his theory that Troy VIh was the victim of an earthquake. The seismic damage to Troy VIh was severe but not catastrophic. Admittedly a number of the palatial houses were ruined and the superstructure of the circuit-wall fell in places, but there is no archaeological evidence to suggest that the fortifications of Troy VIh were actually toppled. Conversely, there is no archaeological evidence to suggest that any of the palatial houses of Troy VIh retained their original function after the earthquake. For these are either left in ruins or divided up, while the wide streets than run between them become cluttered with dismal tenements. In other words, the character of the whole citadel is now so radically different it looks very much as if the ruling elite who resided in houses like House VIM were no longer there. As Wood writes, 'it seems likely that the great houses … ceased to shelter a powerful royal race' (1985: 227). In other words, this dramatic change may be explained by the disappearance of the ruler and his warrior-aristocracy. First weakened by earthquake, there is every reason to believe that Troy VIh was then attacked and sacked by Mycenaean marauders, who removed and processed the survivors – executing some and enslaving others – before putting it to the torch. The era of peace and prosperity, and of the successful rule of a strong citadel, its ships, horses and chariots, was over.

The dates for the destruction of the two levels are much disputed, but it is now likely, as Korfmann (1990: 232) argues, that Troy VIh fell sometime around 1250 BC. This was the time when, at the height of their own power, Mycenaean contacts with Troy were at their most intense. In the aftermath of that destruction, a crowd of people – humbler, but sharing the same material culture as the élites of Troy VIh – moved into the citadel, repairing the fortifications as best they could and building a warren of shanties. This reconstructed, crowded settlement, Troy VIIa, was destroyed sometime around 1180 BC, that is, after the collapse of the Mycenaean civilisation. 'It would appear', says Wood, 'that Troy VIIa *cannot* be Homer's Troy: Troy VIh *could be*' (1985: 225).

It was improbable that the sacking of drab Troy VIIa could have resulted in the *Iliad*, while the apocalyptic end of majestic Troy VIh was never celebrated. The *Iliad* bears evidence of its Mycenaean roots, but as the generations passed successive storytellers may have transformed a polemical drinking-song about an audacious seaborne raid into an epic clash between Asiatic Troy and a unified force of Greek-speaking warriors. The irony in this is a Wooden Horse would take a city famous for taming wild horses. This is a far better tale and it would appeal to the audience, as it has appealed to subsequent generations for some 3,000 years.

The site today

The *Iliad* has made Troy one of the most tangible mythological events in the world and few can resist the chance to tread among its remains. The reality, however, can be less than satisfying. Unless the visitor is well acquainted with the history of the site or has a fertile imagination, the impression given by the present condition of the ruins may be one of disappointment. Considering that nine separate 'cities' of altogether 46 settlement-layers were found on the same spot, as well as the fact that the early excavations were not carried out in a scientific way, the difficulties of understanding the extant ruins of Troy are all too obvious. The visitor, therefore, is strongly advised to arm himself or herself with a good guidebook, such as Korfmann and Mannsperger's *A Guide to Troia*. This publication can be readily purchased from the shop situated at the entrance to the archaeological site.

Situated near the modern village of Truva, the archaeological site of Troy is easily reached from Çanakkale some 30km away. A thriving town on the Asian side of the Dardanelles, which at this point are a little more than 1km wide, Çanakkale has frequent bus services via Bursa and Eceabat to Istanbul, and, via Edremit to Izmir. At the same *otogar* (bus station), some 500m inland from the sea front, you will also find a regular *dolmuş* (minibus) service to Troy. For the return journey you may have to hire a taxi, as the last *dolmuş* often leaves Troy in the mid-afternoon, well before the site closes. The alternative is a 5km hike to the main road, where it is possible to pick up a bus.

Because of its proximity to the battlefields of the Gallipoli campaign, Canakkale has an ample (and varied) selection of hotels and restaurants. The Tourist Information Office near the ferry terminal can advise on accommodation and places to eat, as well as on excursions to the battlefields and Troy.

Troy itself does not possess a museum; however, there is one in Çanakkale. The Archaeological Museum is some 1.5km from the town centre on the main road south towards Troy. Its collections, although not very large, include artefacts from excavated sites in the Troad, including Troy. Objects coming from the various settlement-layers of Troy are well displayed and arranged chronologically, and include some from the Calvert collection.

Useful contact information:

Çanakkale Tourist Information Office
Iskele Meydani 27, 17100 Çanakkale
Tel/Fax: 90 (286) 217 1187
E-mail: canakkale@ttnet.tr

Çanakkale Archaeological Museum
Izmir Caddesi, 17100 Çanakkale
Tel: 90 (286) 217 3252
Fax: 90 (286) 217 1105

Bibliography

The following list is relatively short, and in the main, fairly elementary. Most of the books and articles given below have their own more or less comprehensive bibliographies, which will allow further research into this fascinating subject. One title I thoroughly recommend, and the most readable, by far, is Michael Wood's *In Search of the Trojan War*. For those readers who wish to read Homer himself, there are the fine translations of the two epic poems in verse by Richmond Lattimore and, more recently, Robert Fagles.

Alexander, C., 'Echoes of the Heroic Age', *National Geographic* 185.6, 1999, pp.54–79

Anderson, J. K., 'The Trojan Horse again', *Classical Journal* 66, 1970, pp.22–25

Blegen, C. W., *Troy and the Trojans*, London: Thames and Hudson, 1963

Blegen, C. W., Caskey, J. L., and Rawson, M., *Troy: Excavations Conducted by the University of Cincinnati*, vol. 3, part 1. Princeton: Princeton University Press, 1953

Boedeker, D. (ed.), *The World of Troy: Homer, Schliemann, and the Treasures of Priam*, Washington DC: Society for the Preservation of the Greek Heritage, 1997

Boudreau, E. H., *Making the Adobe Brick*, Berkeley: Fifth Street Press, 1971

Bowra, C. M., 'Homeric Epithets for Troy', *Journal of Hellenic Studies* 80, 1960, pp.16–23

Bryce, T. R., 'Ahhiyawans and Mycenaeans – An Anatolian Viewpoint', *Oxford Journal of Archaeology* 8, 1989, pp.297–310

Calder III, W. M. and Traill, D. A. (eds.), *Myth, Scandal, and History: The Heinrich Schliemann Controversy and a First Edition of the Mycenaean Diary*, Detroit: Wayne State University Press, 1986

Carter, J. B. and Morris, S. P. (eds.), *The Ages of Homer: A Tribute to Emily Townsend Vermeule*, Austin: University of Texas Press, 1995

Chadwick, J., *The Mycenaean World*, Cambridge: Cambridge University Press, 1976

Chadwick, J., *Linear B and Related Scripts*, London: British Museum Publications, 1987

Chadwick, J., *The Decipherment of Linear B*, 2nd edition, Cambridge: Cambridge University Press, 1990

Cook, J. M., *The Troad: An Archaeological and Topographical Study*, Oxford: Clarendon Press, 1973

Dickinson, O. T. P. K., *The Aegean Bronze Age*, Cambridge: Cambridge University Press, 1994

Dörpfeld, W., *Troja und Ilion: Ergebnisse der Ausgrabungen in den vorhistorischen und historischen Schichten von Ilion*, Athens: Barth and von Hirst, 1902

Dossin, G. (ed.), *Archives Royales de Mari*, vol. I, Paris: Impr. Nationale, 1950

Drews, R., *The End of the Bronze Age: Changes in Warfare and the Catastrophe c. 1200 BC*, Princeton: Princeton University Press, 1993

Easton, D. F., 'Has the Trojan War been found?' *Antiquity* 59, 1985, pp.188–96

Easton, D. F., *The Quest for Troy*, London: Weidenfeld and Nicolson, 1997

Fagles, R., *Homer: the Iliad*, London: Penguin, 1991

Fields, N., 'Trojan War', in S. L. Sandler (ed.), *Ground Warfare: An International Encyclopaedia*, Santa Barbara: ABC-CLIO, 2002, 3.896

Finley, M. I., 'The Trojan War', *Journal of Hellenic Studies* 84, 1964, pp.1–20

Finley, M. I., *The World of Odysseus*, 2nd edition, London: Penguin, 1986

Finley, M. I., 'Lost: the Trojan War', in M. I. Finley, *Aspects of Antiquity: Discoveries and Controversies*, London: Penguin, 1991, pp.31–42

Foxhall, L. and Davies, D. K. (eds.), *The Trojan War: Its Historicity and Context – Papers of the First Greenbank Colloquium, Liverpool, 1981*, Bristol: Bristol Classical Press, 1984

Gurney, O. R., *The Hittites*, 2nd edition, London: Penguin, 1990

Güterbock, H. G., 'The Hittites and the Aegean World: 1. The Ahhiyawa problem reconsidered', *American Journal of Archaeology* 87. 1983, pp.133–38

Hunter, L. W. and Handford, S. A., *Aeneas Tacticus on Siegecraft*, Oxford University Press: Oxford, 1927

Jean, C. F. (ed.), *Archives Royales de Mari*, vol. II, Paris: Impr. Nationale, 1950

Korfmann, M., 'Altes und Neues aus Troia', *Das Altertum* 36, 1990, pp.230–40

Korfmann, M. et al., *Traum und Wirklichkeit: Troia*, Stuttgart: Theiss, 2001

Korfmann, M., and Mannsperger, D., *A Guide to Troia*, Istanbul: Ege Press, 1997

Lattimore, R., *The Odyssey of Homer*, London: Harper and Row, 1975

Lattimore, R., *The Iliad of Homer*, Chicago: University of Chicago Press, 1976

Leaf, W., *Troy: A Study in Homeric Geography*, London: Macmillan, 1912

Lorimer, H. L., *Homer and the Monuments*, London: Macmillan, 1950

Luce, J. V., *Homer and the Heroic Age*, London: Thames and Hudson, 1975

Luce, J. V., *Celebrating Homer's Landscapes: Troy and Ithaca Revisited*, Yale: Yale University Press, 1999

Luckenbill, D. D., *Ancient Records of Assyria and Babylonia*, 2 vols, New York: Greenwood Press, 1927

McHenry, P. G., *Adobe: Build it yourself*, Tucson: University of Arizona Press, 1976

Maclaren, C., *The Plain of Troy Described*, Edinburgh: A & C Black, 1863

Macqueen, J. G., *The Hittites and their Contemporaries in Asia Minor*, London: Thames and Hudson, 1986

Mellink, M. J. (ed.), *Troy and the Trojan War: A Symposium held at Bryn Mawr College, October 1984*, Bryn Mawr, Pa.: Bryn Mawr College, 1986

Schliemann, H., *Ilios: The City and Country of the Trojans*, London: John Murray, 1880

Schliemann, H., *Troja: Results of the Latest Researches and Discoveries on the Site of Homer's Troy, 1882*, New York: Benjamin Blom, 1884

Spencer, A. J., *Brick Architecture in Ancient Egypt*, Warminster: Aris and Phillips, 1979

Taylour, W. D., *The Mycenaeans*, 2nd edition, London: Thames and Hudson, 1983

Van Wees, H., *Status Warriors: War, Violence and Society in Homer and History*, Amsterdam: J.C. Gieben, 1992

Ventris, M. G. F. and Chadwick, J., *Documents in Mycenaean Greek*, 2nd edition, Cambridge: Cambridge University Press, 1973

Wachsmann, S., *Seagoing Ships and Seamanship in the Bronze Age Levant*, College Station: Texas A & M University Press, 1998

Wace, A. J. B. and Stubbings, F., *Companion to Homer*, London: Macmillan, 1962

Whitehead, D., *Aineias the Tactician: How to Survive under Siege*, Oxford: Clarendon Press, 1990

Wood, M., *In Search of the Trojan War*, London: BBC Publications, 1985

Yadin, Y., *The Art of Warfare in Biblical Lands: In the Light of Archaeological Discovery*, London: Weidenfeld and Nicolson, 1963

Glossary

An unusually extensive and specialist vocabulary has developed in the field of military architecture. A glossary has therefore been supplied to guide the reader through the technical terms used in the literature covering the fortifications of Troy. Obviously many of the terms below are common to pre-gunpowder fortifications in general.

ashlar – worked stone with flat surface, usually of regular shape and square edges

bastion – structural rather than inhabitable and generally serving as a fighting platform

batter – the receding slope of the exterior face of the stone portion of a curtain-wall

cistern – storage place for potable water

crenellation – fortified parapet, complete with merlons and crenels, at the top of a curtain-wall

curtain – main wall of a defensive work or the part of a rampart hung between two contiguous towers

Cyclopean – drystone masonry of huge blocks or boulders

enceinte – area enclosed within a citadel's main line of ramparts, but excluding its outworks

header – a stone block laid across a wall so that its end is flush with the outer surface (cf. stretcher)

mortar – a mixture of clay and water used to bind stones together, as opposed to dry-laid masonry

offset – vertical indentation in a curtain-wall that allows a slight change in direction

parapet – low, narrow, defensive wall, usually with crenels (open part) and merlons (closed part), along the upper outer edge of a curtain-wall

polygonal – drystone masonry of large roughly worked blocks

postern – small additional gateway

stretcher – a stone block laid horizontally with its length parallel to the length of a wall (cf. header)

wall-walk – walkway, usually protected by a parapet, along the top of a curtain-wall

Appendix I: Homeric epithets for Troy

In the Homeric epics cities need epithets as much as gods and heroes do, and Troy is certainly no exception. Indeed, Troy has epithets that are always consistent with its site and appearance and often illuminating and picturesque.

Strong-founded/ Well-built	*Iliad* 1.164, 2.133, 4.33, 5.489, 8.288, 9.402, 13.380, 21.433 etc.
Strong-walled	*Iliad* 1.129, 2.113, 288, 5. 716, 8.241, 9.20, *Odyssey* 20.302 etc.
Strong-towered	*Iliad* 7.71, 16.700, 22.195
Gate-towering	*Iliad* 16.698, 21.544
Impregnable	*Iliad* 21.447
Wide-wayed	*Iliad* 2.12, 29, 66, 141, 9.28, 14.88, *Odyssey* 22.230 etc.
Great	*Iliad* 2.332, 803, 6.392, 7.296, 9.136, 22.251, *Odyssey* 3.108 etc.
Sacred/Hallowed	*Iliad* 4.46, 164, 416, 5.648, 6.96, 277, 448, 8.551, *Odyssey* 1.2 etc.
Beautiful/Elegant	*Iliad* 5.210, 22.121
Steep/Sheer	*Iliad* 9.419, 13.625, 17.327, *Odyssey* 3.130, 11.533, 13.316 etc.
Windy	*Iliad* 3.305, 8.499, 12.115, 13.724, 18.175, 23.64, 297

Index